MONEYHOPE.LIFE SERIES BOOK 1

YOUR MONEY IDENTITY

VIRGINIA N DVORAK

Your Money Identity

MANHATTAN
BOOK GROUP
Published by Manhattan Book Group
447 Broadway 2nd Floor, #354, New York, NY 10013
(212) 634-7677 | www.manhattanbookgroup.com
Printed in the United States of America

ISBN-13: 978-1-972090-87-9 (Paperback)
ISBN-13: 978-1-972090-88-6 (Hardcover)

I dedicate this to my children, Amanda and Robert.

TABLE OF CONTENTS

INTRODUCTION

People yearn for financial freedom.

> We spend money we don't have or haven't earned, to buy things we don't need, to impress people we do not like.
>
> —Will Rogers and others have said things similar to this.

I wrote this moneyhope.life book series to equip people. Because:

- Most people at all income levels live paycheck to paycheck. With no emergency fund, they are one flat tire or one medical expense from a financial crisis.
- Money is a life skill that can be learned at any age, but life is greatly enhanced if learned early.
- There are thousands of books that are one-dimensional. They are either a "how to" guide, with no principles which are needed for lasting effects, or they are based on "principles" with no link to what

it looks like or how to do it. The Moneyhope.life book series is different.

The Moneyhope.life book series gives readers:

- Tools to enhance their relationship to money,
- Stories to bring them hope and, at the same time,
- Skills to enhance the rest of their life.

The moneyhope.life book series is for new adults to learn money and life skills to make their lives easier and more complete. The books also have information so readers of any age can gain knowledge and peace of mind. I know people of all ages with overwhelming debt which keeps them from having financial freedom and enjoying experiences they would love to have. The books introduce readers to real-life circumstances and offer money and life skills to turn bad situations into positive opportunities.

I have had years of experience as a Certified Public Accountant with an MBA in Finance and years mentoring high school girls. I grew up with a lack of financial resources and it affected my security and sense of self-worth for many years. I want to equip young people to thrive in our modern social media influencer society where it is so easy to compare ourselves to images and lives you see on a screen. My thoughts about money have been influenced by my life experiences, my education, my life-skills, working with young women and wisdom which I have received from reading and studying books about money as well as from ancient wisdom in the Old (Torah) and New Testaments of the Bible, which are still relevant today.

The Moneyhope.life book series consists of five books. They build on each other and go step by step getting deeper each time.

- Books 1 and 2 are about the **Heart**.
- Book 3 is about the **Mind**.
- Book 4 is about the **Soul**.
- Book 5 is about **Relationships.**

Book 1: Your Money Identity

This kicks off the series with "The Question That Changes Everything."

- Our needs for "Significance, Comfort and Control", impact how we think about ourselves and how they impact our money decisions.
- We should not compare ourselves to others, our prior expectations (a middle-class lifestyle that is better than our parent's lifestyles, big HGTV houses, fabulous vacations, brand name possessions) and, we need to understand lifestyle inflation.
- By working hard some people can have money and possessions and may think they deserve it, however, many people work just as hard or harder and cannot have the same possessions – therefore it is not about "deserving".
- Emotions, the concept of having "enough", FOMO (fear of missing out), self-worth, gratitude, generosity, service, temptation, wants vs. needs, having a poverty or accumulation mindset, contentment and

lasting gratification via delayed gratification are all covered in the book.

- There are practical strategies for each of the topics as well as including people with different circumstances, those at different life stages and those with different learning styles.

Author's note: The purpose of this book is to inform people about money and life. It is written for people of all faiths as well as those who do not have any religious faith. Whatever your beliefs, there is ancient wisdom about finances that still holds true today. The book draws on a wide variety of sources from both the Old and New Testaments of the Bible. Unless otherwise noted, the references in this book are to the NIV ("New International Standard Version") translation of the Bible. All information that is from the Bible is clearly marked in the text.

THE QUESTION THAT CHANGES EVERYTHING

What is your relationship with money? It's a question most of us never pause to consider, yet the answer shapes nearly every aspect of our lives. Money affects our health care decisions, our educational choices, our sense of justice and liberty, and, yes, even our pursuit of happiness. It also affects those around us and even the natural environment. Whether we realize it or not, money is woven into the fabric of our daily existence, influencing not only what we buy but also who we believe ourselves to be – our money identity.

The truth is, we all have a money identity—a deep-seated belief system about money that drives our financial decisions, often without our conscious awareness. This identity was formed long before we earned our first paycheck. It is shaped by our sense of self-worth, along with childhood experiences, family attitudes, cultural messages, and life circumstances that teach us what money means and what it can do for us.

Author's note: My two children, raised together in the same house, have different money identities.

For some, money represents security—a shield against life's uncertainties. For others, it symbolizes success, status, or self-worth. Many see it as a tool for comfort or control. Still others view it with suspicion, fear, or shame. But here's what most of us miss: our money identity, more than our actual financial circumstances, determines whether we experience financial peace or financial bondage.

We start with the most profound question. This question isn't just about money; the way each of us answers it affects how we see ourselves, what our priorities are, and how we think about money. This book will help you understand and mold your financial identity. Only then will you be able to have financial freedom and be in control of your money and thus, your life.

CHAPTER 1

The Three Deadly Desires

At the core of most financial struggles lie three fundamental desires that, while natural and even healthy in moderation, can become destructive when they drive our financial decisions. These are the desires for **significance, comfort,** and **control.** Understanding these desires—how they work, why they're so powerful, and how they manifest in our daily financial choices—is crucial for anyone seeking financial peace and authentic living.

Think of these three desires as invisible forces constantly pulling at your wallet. They whisper promises in your ear: "Buy this, and you'll finally feel important." "Purchase that, and you'll be comfortable." "Acquire this, and you'll have control over your life." But like sirens calling sailors to shipwreck, these voices often lead us away from our true financial destination toward the rocks of debt, anxiety, and spiritual emptiness.

- *Debt is regret—it robs you of your future.*
- *Save first—then buy.*

The Desire for Significance: When Your Worth Becomes Your Net Worth

- *We spend money we don't have, or haven't earned, to buy things we don't need, to impress people we don't like.*

Who are we trying to impress? Why them? Are they really the ones who matter? Do they accept us for who we are?

Understand the Power of the Significance Drive

The desire for significance is perhaps the most expensive of the three deadly desires because it's never satisfied. It manifests as the need to achieve status through what we own, where we live, how we appear to others, and what brands we associate with our identity. This desire asks the dangerous question: "What will people think?"

If you are fairly young, this desire hits particularly hard. You're in the life stage where you're establishing your adult identity, building your career, and often comparing yourself to peers who seem to have it all figured out. Social media amplifies this exponentially—every day you see carefully curated glimpses of others' lives that make your own seem lacking.

This does affect those in midlife and older as well. You may be reflecting on where you are compared with your previous expectations. Does it compare or contrast? Does it matter that it doesn't look like your previous expectation? Just because your current circumstance is different from what you imagined you wanted doesn't mean your present circumstance is not fine. Who do you compare yourself with? Do you still have goals that you want to accomplish in the next phases of your life?

VIP ("Very Important Person")—Many establishments offer us the "opportunity" to be "VIPs." I have recently been thinking that I oppose the concept of "VIPs." It just nourishes the power of significance. I can pay to be a VIP at my bookstore. Does that make me feel special? Now, I decline opportunities to pay more for a "VIP" status, which is fake anyway.

Picture This

Imagine your identity as a house. When significance drives your financial decisions, you're constantly renovating the exterior to impress passersby while the foundation crumbles underneath. The house looks impressive from the street—designer furniture visible through the windows, a luxury car in the driveway, the latest gadgets displayed on counters. But inside, the structure is weak because all the money went to appearances rather than substance.

Now picture a different house: a modest exterior, an older but well-maintained car, but inside you find solid construction, an emergency fund "foundation," investment accounts growing like strong support beams, and the peace that comes with living below your means. Which house would you rather actually live in?

The Psychology Behind Significance

Psychologists call this "conspicuous consumption," spending designed to signal status to others. But here's the trap: the people you're trying to impress are often too busy trying to impress others to notice your efforts. Meanwhile, the people who truly matter—those who love you regardless of what you own—may actually be concerned about the financial stress your image-building is creating.

The significance trap is cruel because of the following:

- **Career pressure:** You feel you need to "look successful" to advance professionally.
- **Dating dynamics:** There's pressure to appear financially attractive to potential partners.
- **Social circles:** Friend groups often revolve around expensive activities and experiences.
- **Family expectations:** Parents or relatives may have certain lifestyle expectations based on their life experience or priorities.
- **Middle-class expectations:** There was real growth among middle-class families after World War II, but over the last fifty years, this has changed. Previously, people expected their children to be better off than they had been. This may no longer be the case. Recent polls show that many US adults no longer believe in

the American dream, and some believe that it was never really true.

- **Digital comparison:** Social Media such as Instagram, TikTok, and LinkedIn are designed to create constant comparison opportunities.

Authentic Success Versus Performed Success

The pursuit of significance through possessions often conflicts with authentic personal values. Many people report feeling exhausted by the constant pressure to maintain an image, especially when that image doesn't reflect their true priorities or financial reality.

Research in positive psychology shows that intrinsic motivations (personal growth, relationships, contribution to community) lead to greater life satisfaction than extrinsic motivations (wealth, fame, image). When your financial decisions are driven by significance-seeking, you're essentially choosing extrinsic motivations that research shows will leave you less satisfied.

Questions for Reflection

- What would your spending look like if no one could see your purchases?
- How much of your income goes toward impressing others versus supporting your actual values?
- When you make purchases to impress others, whose approval are you really seeking?
- How do you reconcile wanting to "look successful" with teachings about humility?

- Which purchases have brought you genuine satisfaction versus temporary status pleasure?
- How might living more simply actually be a form of worship and trust in God's provision?

The desire for significance through possessions directly conflicts with wisdom about identity. Our worth comes from our purpose, which is the purpose of our beliefs.

Real-World Examples of Significance-Driven Spending

The Fresh Graduate: JN just landed her first "real job," making forty-five thousand dollars. Instead of building an emergency fund, she finances a car that costs thirty-five thousand to look successful to colleagues and friends. The monthly payment, insurance, and maintenance consume 40 percent of her take-home pay, leaving no room for savings or unexpected expenses.

The Social Media Influencer: OS works in green energy and earns good money, but he spends most of it on experiences and items that photograph well—expensive restaurants, designer clothes, exotic vacations. His Instagram looks amazing, but he has fifteen grand in credit card debt and no retirement savings.

The Family Pressure Case: AL feels pressure from her successful family to maintain a certain lifestyle. She rents an expensive apartment in the "right" neighborhood and shops at stores her family approves of, even though it means living paycheck to paycheck and borrowing money for basic expenses.

The True Cost of Significance-Seeking

The financial cost of significance-seeking is obvious: overspending, debt, and a lack of savings. But the hidden costs are often more devastating. It can be like trying to fill up a bottomless pit—never coming close to having enough.

Emotional Costs

- Constant anxiety about maintaining the image.
- Fear of being "found out" as financially struggling.
- Exhaustion from keeping up appearances.
- Reduced authentic relationships (people drawn to your image, not your true self).

Opportunity Costs

- Money spent on image could have been invested for future security.
- Time spent maintaining appearances could have been used for personal growth.
- Energy focused on others' opinions could have been directed toward meaningful goals.

Relational Costs

- Difficulty forming authentic connections when you're always performing.
- Financial stress affecting romantic relationships.

- Inability to be generous because all money goes to self-promotion, or conversely being so generous that your own needs are not met.
- Modeling poor financial values for younger siblings or future children.

Strategies to Overcome Significance-Seeking

Create Comparison Charts

Make two columns: "Image Purchases" and "Value Purchases." Track your spending for a month and categorize each purchase. Which column brings more lasting satisfaction?

The Voice Test

Before making a purchase, ask aloud: "*Am I buying this for me or for others to see?*" If you can't honestly say it's for you, wait 48 hours before purchasing. Another question to ask is, "*What if I buy this and it gets lost or stolen? Can I really afford it?*" If you cannot afford to lose it, don't buy it.

The Physical Purge

Remember—our stuff owns us. Some people have so much stuff that they don't even have a place to put it—and they spend more money to put it in storage. Go through your possessions and physically separate items into "truly useful/loved" and "bought for image." Get rid of everything that isn't useful, beautiful, or joyful. Close the storage unit.

Donate or sell the image items and notice how little you actually miss them.

Journal Prompts

- "When I imagine not owning [expensive item], what emotion comes up?"
- "Who am I trying to impress and why does their opinion matter to me?"
- "What would I spend money on if no one could see my purchases?"

Build Authentic Confidence

True significance comes from developing actual competence, contributing meaningfully to others, and aligning your actions with your values—none of which require expensive purchases.

Competence Building

- Invest in education, skills, and experiences that genuinely make you more capable.
- Choose purchases that support your actual goals rather than your image goals.
- Build expertise in areas you're passionate about, regardless of how they appear to others.

Contribution Focus

- Redirect a portion of "image spending" toward helping others.
- Volunteer time instead of spending money to feel important.
- Use your skills to solve problems for family, friends, or the community.

Values Alignment

- Identify your core values (family, growth, creativity, justice, etc.).
- Examine your spending to see how much actually supports those values.
- Make financial decisions that reflect who you want to be, not who you want others to think you are.

The Desire for Comfort: When More Stuff Equals Less Satisfaction

Understand the Comfort Trap

The desire for comfort manifests as the belief that having more money will make us happier, safer, or more satisfied. It whispers: "If you just had a bigger house, a newer car, fancier vacations, then you'd finally be content." This desire seems reasonable—who doesn't want to be comfortable?—but it creates what psychologists call the "hedonic treadmill."

Here's how the treadmill works: You get a promotion and can afford a nicer apartment. Initially, the upgrade feels amazing. But within a few months, you've adapted to the new normal, and now you're eyeing an even better place. The comfort that once satisfied you now feels insufficient. You're running faster and faster on the treadmill but not actually getting anywhere.

The Science of Satisfaction

Research consistently shows that beyond meeting basic needs (housing, food, health care, transportation), additional income provides diminishing returns on happiness. The magic number varies by location, but studies suggest that emotional well-being plateaus around $75,000–$100,000 annually in most US areas.

This doesn't mean money doesn't matter—it means that once you can cover necessities plus some discretionary spending, the happiness you gain from each additional dollar decreases dramatically. Yet most people continue to believe that the next level of comfort will finally bring lasting satisfaction.

The Comfort Curve

Picture a graph where the x-axis represents income/possessions and the y-axis represents happiness. The line rises steeply at first (meeting basic needs creates significant happiness gains), then levels off (comfort zone), and eventually becomes almost flat (additional comfort barely registers).

Most people focus on moving further right on the x-axis (more stuff) rather than understanding they're already in the zone where additional movement provides minimal benefit. They're chasing diminishing returns instead of investing in what actually sustains happiness: relationships, purpose, health, and personal growth.

Comfort-Seeking in Different Life Stages

As we go through life, the way we think about having comfort changes. The things we want in order to have a comfortable lifestyle also change.

The Setup Phase
Fresh graduates often go into debt to furnish apartments, buy professional wardrobes, and create the lifestyle they think successful adults should have. The comfort-seeking question becomes: "What do I need to feel like a real adult?"

The Upgrade Phase
As income increases, so do comfort expectations. The studio apartment feels cramped, the used car feels embarrassing, and the basic wardrobe feels insufficient. Each upgrade promises to be "the last one," but never is.

The Lifestyle Inflation Phase
Higher salaries get absorbed into higher expenses. What once felt luxurious (eating out twice a week) becomes routine. New luxuries (organic everything, premium gym memberships, regular travel) become the new normal.

The Downsizing Phase

You may not think about it now, but at some point, you may realize that you don't need as much stuff. The stuff can become a burden—either crowding your living space or costing money to store.

Contentment as a Learned Discipline

There is much in the Bible about contentment and the pursuit of comfort. Paul writes, "I have learned to be content whatever the circumstances" (Philippians 4:11). Notice he says "learned"—contentment is a skill developed through practice, not a feeling that arrives automatically with better circumstances.

Jesus warned against the comfort trap: "Watch out! Be on your guard against all kinds of greed; life does not consist in an abundance of possessions" (Luke 12:15). The parable that follows tells of a rich man who built bigger barns to store his surplus, thinking this would give him security and comfort, only to die that very night.

The concept of contentment doesn't mean accepting injustice or never working to improve your situation. It means finding peace and gratitude in your current circumstances while taking wise action toward appropriate goals. It means recognizing that your comfort and security ultimately do not come from accumulating stuff.

Principles for Comfort-Seeking

- Godliness with contentment is great gain (1 Timothy 6:6).

- Seek first his kingdom and his righteousness, and all these things will be given to you as well (Matthew 6:33).
- The love of money is a root of all kinds of evil (1 Timothy 6:10).
- Keep your life free from love of money and be content with what you have (Hebrews 13:5).

The Psychology of Enough

Understanding the psychology of comfort-seeking can lead to more satisfying financial decisions. Behavioral economists have identified several cognitive biases that fuel the comfort trap:

Adaptation Theory: We quickly adapt to positive changes in our circumstances, returning to baseline happiness levels despite improved conditions.

Social Comparison Theory: Our satisfaction depends more on relative status than absolute comfort levels.

Choice Overload: Having more options (which money provides) can actually decrease satisfaction rather than increase it.

The Paradox of Choice: When we have unlimited options, we're more likely to regret our decisions and wonder if we chose wrong.

The Real Costs of Comfort-Seeking

Financial Costs

- Lifestyle inflation consumes pay raises, preventing wealth building.
- Comfort purchases often depreciate rapidly (cars, furniture, electronics).
- The "comfort lifestyle" requires ongoing expenses that become fixed costs.
- Emergency fund money gets redirected to comfort upgrades.

Psychological Costs

- Decreased satisfaction as adaptation kicks in.
- Increased anxiety about maintaining the comfort level.
- Decision fatigue from constantly evaluating upgrade options.
- Regret and buyer's remorse when comfort purchases don't deliver promised satisfaction.

Social Costs

- Less money available for generosity and helping others.
- Difficulty relating to friends with different income levels.
- Modeling consumption-focused values for others.

- Reduced time for relationships due to working more to afford comfort.

Strategies for Managing Comfort Desires

We all want to be comfortable. Being comfortable allows us to pursue higher dreams and goals for our lives. Here are ways to manage the drive for comfort.

The Gratitude Practice

Before making any comfort-upgrade purchase, spend one week actively appreciating what you currently have. For visual learners, photograph aspects of your current situation you're grateful for. For auditory learners, verbally express gratitude daily. For kinesthetic learners, physically interact with items you already own and notice their positive qualities.

The Future Self Exercise

Write a letter to yourself one year from now describing the comfort purchase you're considering. Ask your future self: "Did this upgrade actually improve my life in lasting ways?" Most honest future selves report that the upgrade mattered much less than expected.

The Service Experiment

Instead of spending money on comfort upgrades, volunteer time helping people with fewer resources. This recalibrates your perspective on what constitutes "enough" and often provides more lasting satisfaction than purchases.

The Thirty-Day Rule

When you want to make a comfort upgrade, wait thirty days. During this time, actively notice whether the lack of the upgrade actually affects your daily happiness. Most people discover they stop thinking about the desired item within a week.

Find Sustainable Comfort

True comfort comes from security, not luxury. Security means

- having an emergency fund for unexpected expenses;
- living below your means so money stress doesn't dominate your thoughts;
- investing in appreciating assets rather than depreciating comfort items; and
- building skills and relationships that provide non-monetary security.

Sustainable Comfort Principles

1. **Quality over Quantity:** Buy fewer, better things that last longer.
2. **Function over Form:** Prioritize items that genuinely improve your life over items that just look impressive.
3. **Experience over Objects:** Research shows experiences provide more lasting satisfaction than possessions.
4. **Relationship over Acquisition:** Invest in people and experiences that strengthen relationships.

The Desire for Control: When Money Becomes Your Sense of Security

Does money make us feel safe? Does it provide us with security? It may seem so if we go from having no emergency savings to having some. However, there is more to the feeling of being in control than the amount of cash we have access to.

Understand the Control Illusion

The desire for control reveals itself in our belief that money can provide security and predictability in an uncertain world. We think that a fat bank account will protect us from life's storms, that financial resources equal personal power, and that having more gives us more options and, therefore, more control over our circumstances.

- *Many people do not have a realistic understanding of financial risk, nor do they have an emergency fund.*
- *Most people feel powerless over their finances.*

This desire feels entirely reasonable. Having money does provide some security and options. An emergency fund can cover unexpected medical bills. Savings can allow you to leave a bad job. Investments can provide retirement security. The problem isn't wanting financial security—the problem is believing that enough money can provide complete security and control.

The Control Paradox

Here's the paradox: the more we rely on money for control and security, the more anxious and out of control we often feel. Why?

1. **There's never "enough" for complete security:** No matter how much you save, you can imagine scenarios that would require more.
2. **Markets are unpredictable:** Investments can lose value, and job security can disappear overnight.
3. **Health and relationships can't be purchased:** The most important aspects of security (health, love, meaning) aren't fully within our control, even with money.
4. **The fear of loss grows with accumulation:** The more you have, the more you have to lose.

The Security Illusion

Imagine security as a medieval castle. Money allows you to build higher walls, deeper moats, and stronger gates. But no castle is impregnable, and the effort spent building ever-stronger defenses can consume so much time and energy that you never actually enjoy the safety you've created.

Now imagine security as a well-tended garden. Instead of building walls against all possible threats, you develop resilience—multiple income streams like diverse crops, skills like fertile soil, and relationships like beneficial insects that support the ecosystem. This garden may not look as defensively impressive as a castle, but it's often more sustainable and satisfying to inhabit.

Control-Seeking Behaviors

The Scarcity Saver: EM makes good money but keeps everything in low-interest savings accounts because investing feels too risky. She has fifty grand earning 0.5 percent because she's afraid of losing any of it, even though inflation is eroding its purchasing power every year.

The Multiple Income Hustler: JO works his full-time job, drives for rideshare services evenings and weekends, sells products online, and constantly looks for more income streams. He believes more money means more security, but he's exhausted and has no time for relationships or personal care.

The Insurance Maximizer: LI purchases every possible insurance policy and warranty to be "protected against everything." She spends so much on insurance premiums that she can't build actual wealth, making her more financially vulnerable, not less.

The Luxury Hoarder: MC grew up poor, and now that he earns good money, he accumulates expensive items "just in case." His apartment is full of things he never uses but bought because "you never know when you might need it."

Trust Versus Self-Reliance

The Bible addresses the desire for control directly, particularly the tendency to trust in riches rather than in God. Proverbs 11:28 warns: "Those who trust in their riches will fall, but the righteous will thrive like a green leaf."

Jesus taught extensively about worry and control, particularly in Matthew 6:25–34: "Do not worry about your life, what you will eat or drink, or about your body, what you will wear... But seek first his kingdom and his righteousness and all these things will be given to you as well."

This doesn't mean that we should be financially irresponsible or never save money. Scripture also teaches about being wise stewards (Luke 14:28–30) and planning ahead (Proverbs 21:5). The key is the difference between wise financial planning and anxious attempts to control outcomes through accumulation.

Reflection Questions

- When do your financial plans reflect wise stewardship versus anxious control-seeking?
- How do you balance saving for the future with trusting God's provision?
- What fears drive your financial decisions, and what do those fears reveal?

Risk Management Versus Risk Avoidance

The desire for control through money often stems from evolutionary survival instincts that don't serve us well in modern financial contexts. Our brains are wired to fear loss more than we value equivalent gains (loss aversion), to overestimate rare but dramatic risks while underestimating common but gradual risks.

Modern financial planning is about managing risk, not eliminating it. The attempt to eliminate all financial risk often creates more risk by:

- Not increasing your lifetime earnings potential by investing in quality education in a field that leads to higher earning career opportunities (career optimization).
- Keeping too much money in low-yield accounts (inflation risk).
- Avoiding investments that could outpace inflation (opportunity cost risk).
- Working excessive hours for current income instead of building skills (career stagnation risk).
- Focusing only on financial security while neglecting health and relationships (life satisfaction risk).

The Myth of Financial Control

Market Reality: Stock markets, real estate values, interest rates, and job markets are influenced by global events, government policies, technological changes, and countless other factors beyond any individual's control.

Health Reality: Medical emergencies can occur despite the best insurance and healthiest lifestyle. Chronic illnesses can develop regardless of financial preparation.

Career Reality: Industries can become obsolete, companies can downsize, and skills can become outdated faster than ever before.

Life Reality: Relationships, natural disasters, family circumstances, and personal changes can all affect financial situations in unpredictable ways.

Healthy Financial Control Versus Anxiety-Driven Control

What is the difference between having a healthy level of financial control and one that causes you fear and anxiety? Here are examples:

Healthy Financial Control Looks Like

- Building an emergency fund sized appropriately for your situation (3–6 months of expenses).
- Diversifying investments across different asset classes and risk levels.
- Lifelong learning by developing multiple skills that make you more employable.
- Maintaining good relationships that provide emotional and sometimes practical support.
- Taking care of your physical and mental health.
- Having adequate but not excessive insurance coverage.

Anxiety-Driven Control Looks Like

- Working in low-paying jobs without investing in your financial future.
- Hoarding cash in low-yield accounts far beyond reasonable emergency fund levels.
- Avoiding all investments due to fear of loss.
- Working excessive hours to accumulate money while sacrificing health and relationships.
- Buying excessive insurance or warranties for peace of mind.
- Making financial decisions primarily based on worst-case scenarios.
- Being unable to be generous because "you never know what might happen."

Strategies for Managing Control Desires

So, how? What are ways to actually manage our need for control?

The Scenario Planning Exercise

Instead of trying to prepare for every possible financial catastrophe, identify the three most likely challenges you might face (job loss, medical expense, car repair, etc.). Create specific, realistic plans for these scenarios, which provides actual security rather than vague anxiety.

The Control Review

List your current financial strategies and honestly assess: "Is this about reasonable preparation or anxiety management?" If you're spending more on managing financial anxiety than on building your finances, it's time to rebalance.

The Gratitude for Uncertainty Practice

This sounds counterintuitive, but uncertainty also creates opportunities. The same unpredictability that makes jobs disappear also creates new career possibilities. The same market volatility that can cause losses can also create gains. Practice acknowledging that uncertainty brings both risks and opportunities.

The Resilience Building Focus

Instead of trying to control outcomes, focus on building resilience—your ability to adapt and recover from setbacks. This might mean the following:

- Research future career opportunities and the financial benefits of education.
- Developing multiple income-generating skills.
- Building strong relationships that provide support during difficult times.
- Maintaining physical and mental health.
- Cultivating spiritual or philosophical resources that provide meaning during challenges.
- Building a diverse network of contacts and opportunities.

Integration: How the Three Desires Work Together

These three desires, significance, comfort, and control, rarely operate in isolation. More often, they work together to create perfect storms of financial dysfunction. Understanding how they interact helps explain why changing financial behavior can be so challenging and why surface-level budgeting advice often fails. They are sometimes called the vicious cycle. Here are common combinations to watch out for:

Significance + Comfort: You buy expensive items to impress others *and* because you believe they'll make you happier. The result? Maximum financial damage for minimal lasting benefit.

Comfort + Control: You upgrade your lifestyle for comfort *and* convince yourself it's really about security. "I need transportation" becomes a justification for a luxury vehicle with expensive payments.

Significance + Control: You accumulate wealth to impress others *and* to feel secure. This can lead to becoming wealthy but miserable, focused entirely on accumulation rather than enjoyment or generosity.

Significance + Comfort + Control (All Three Together): This creates financial behavior that's simultaneously expensive (significance), never satisfying (comfort), and anxiety-provoking (control). You're spending money you don't have, or haven't earned, on things you don't need, to impress people you don't like—all while worrying constantly about your financial security.

Break the Cycle

Now that we understand the three deadly desires and how they impact our lives and money, what can we do to make lasting change? Here are some thoughts.

Recognition: The first step to breaking the cycle is recognizing which desires drive your financial decisions. Most people have one primary driver with the others playing supporting roles. Identifying your primary driver allows you to be aware of "it" when "it" tries to influence your decisions.

Alternative Satisfaction: Once you know what is driving your desire, you can look for alternatives. I suggest you find ways to meet these legitimate needs without expensive purchases. You can create a feeling of Significance through your own competence and contribution. You can find comfort by expressing gratitude or by working on relationships with friends, family, coworkers, or others in your community. Control can be achieved through personal resilience and planning.

Values Alignment: After finding alternative ways to satisfy your needs, you can practice values alignment. Make financial decisions based on your stated values rather than these subconscious desires. If family is important to you, how do your financial choices support family relationships? If creativity matters to you, how does your spending reflect that priority? If sustainability is important to you, how is your spending affecting the planet and the rest of us?

Community Support: Lastly, it is easier to accomplish these goals with community support. Surround yourself with people who share your financial values rather than people who enable your financially destructive desires.

The Path Forward

The three deadly desires aren't evil in themselves—they become problems when they drive financial decisions without conscious awareness. Significance, comfort, and control are legitimate human needs. The question is: How will you meet these needs in ways that support rather than undermine your overall well-being?

Here are ways to create healthy significance, comfort, and control:

Healthy Significance comes from developing real competence, contributing meaningfully to others, and living authentically in line with your values.

Healthy Comfort comes from gratitude for what you have, security in your relationships and skills, and spending money on things that genuinely align with your priorities.

Healthy Control comes from building resilience, making wise preparations for likely challenges, and accepting that ultimate control isn't possible or even desirable.

The journey toward financial health begins with understanding these desires, recognizing how they manifest in your own life, and choosing to meet them in ways that build rather than destroy your long-term well-being. This isn't about eliminating normal human desires—it's about fulfilling them wisely.

Conclusion Chapter One

At the core of most financial struggles lie three fundamental desires that, while natural, can become destructive when they drive our financial decisions. These are the desires for significance, comfort, and control.

The Desire for Significance manifests as the need to achieve status through what we own, where we live, or how we appear to others. We get our identity from job titles, possessions, lifestyle, and brand names. We find ourselves asking: "What will people think if I drive this car, live in this neighborhood, or wear these clothes?" This desire drives us to spend money we don't have on things we don't need to impress people who ultimately don't matter to our true well-being.

💡 *Debt is regret—it robs you of your future.*

💡 *Save first—then buy.*

The Desire for Comfort shows up as the belief that having more money will make us happier, safer, or more satisfied. We tell ourselves that if we just had a little more—a bigger house, a newer car, fancier vacations—then we'd finally be content. But research consistently shows that beyond meeting our basic needs, additional income provides diminishing returns on happiness. The comfortable lifestyle we chase often becomes a trap that keeps us working longer hours, taking on more debt, and sacrificing relationships for financial gain.

When most people receive an increase in their wages, they increase their expenses and still end up without financial freedom. This is called lifestyle creep or lifestyle inflation.

The Desire for Control reveals itself in our belief that money can provide security and predictability in an uncertain world. We think that a fat bank account will protect us from life's storms, that financial resources equal personal power, and that having more gives us more options and, therefore, more control over our circumstances. While money can certainly provide some security, the illusion of control it offers often leads to anxiety, hoarding, and the fear of never having enough.

Most people feel powerless over their finances.

Many people do not have a realistic understanding of financial risk, nor do they have an emergency fund.

Unfortunately for all of us, these desires often work together to become even more powerful and less obvious. You can't make these desires go away—they're part of human nature. The problem comes when these desires begin to define us, when our identity becomes so intertwined with our financial status that we can't separate our worth as a person from our net worth as an account holder. The solution is taking control by recognizing these desires and fulfilling them in healthy, lasting ways.

In the next chapter, we'll explore how these desires create specific mindsets that keep people trapped in financial struggle and, more importantly, how to transform those mindsets into ones that support financial peace and authentic living.

CHAPTER 2

The Mindset Trap

As he thinks in his heart, so is he.

—Proverbs 23:7 NKJV
("New King James Version")

Understand the Power of Mindset

Imagine two people, both earning forty-five thousand dollars a year, both living in the same city. SH constantly worries about money, feels she never has enough, and makes financial decisions out of fear and scarcity. Meanwhile, JK feels grateful for what he has, makes thoughtful spending choices, and believes he can improve his financial situation over time. Same income, same circumstances—but completely different financial realities.

The difference? Their mindsets.

Your mindset isn't just how you think about money—it's the lens through which you see every financial opportunity, challenge, and decision. It's the internal operating system that runs in the background of your consciousness, influencing choices you make without even realizing it.

See it: Think of mindset like the filter on your camera phone. The same scene can look warm and inviting with one filter, dark and depressing with another. Your money mindset is the filter through which you view every financial situation.

Feel it: Mindset is like the current in a river. You might not always see it or feel it directly, but it's constantly pushing you in a particular direction. Swimming against a strong current is exhausting; swimming with it makes progress feel effortless.

Hear it: Consider mindset as the background music in a movie. It sets the emotional tone for every scene. Scary music makes even mundane situations feel threatening, while uplifting music makes challenges feel conquerable.

The Three Destructive Mindsets

Your current financial struggles may have less to do with your income level than with your money mindset. Let's explore the three most common and destructive thought patterns that keep people trapped in financial bondage, regardless of how much they earn.

The Poverty Mindset

The poverty mindset means you fear living in scarcity—not having enough. This anxiety takes your peace of mind and can feel overwhelming, even when it is not rational based on your circumstances.

What It Looks Like

The poverty mindset is like wearing glasses that make everything appear smaller, scarcer, and more threatening than it actually is. It keeps you focused on what you don't have, convincing you that there will never be enough. This scarcity thinking creates a cycle of worry, fear, and sometimes self-sabotage that becomes a self-fulfilling prophecy.

Real-Life Examples

- **MY, college graduate:** Despite landing a decent entry-level job, she constantly says "I can't afford that" even for small purchases she could easily manage. She grew up hearing her parents argue about money and now assumes financial stress is inevitable.
- **DV, plumber:** He avoids investing because he's convinced that he'll lose money. He keeps all his savings in a checking account earning 0.1 percent interest because it "feels safer," even though inflation is eroding his purchasing power every year.
- **JE, marketing coordinator:** She turns down professional development opportunities because she can't bear to spend money on courses or conferences, even though these investments could significantly increase her earning potential.

The Internal Dialogue

- "There's never enough money."
- "I don't deserve nice things."
- "Rich people are just lucky—that'll never be me."
- "If I spend money on this, something bad will happen."
- "I need to save every penny for emergencies" (but then feels guilty about any spending).

How It Develops

The poverty mindset often starts in childhood, but it can develop at any age through traumatic financial experiences. Maybe you grew up in a household where money was always tight, where financial stress was a constant presence. Perhaps your parents experienced job loss, foreclosure, or bankruptcy. Or maybe you've experienced your own financial setbacks that created deep-seated fears about money.

You might have grown up hearing that "money is the root of all evil" (a misquote of 1 Timothy 6:10, which actually says "the *love* of money is a root of all kinds of evil"). Some faith communities inadvertently promote poverty mindsets by suggesting that financial struggle is more spiritual or that wanting financial security shows a lack of faith, which creates internal conflict between practical financial needs and spiritual identity.

Have you absorbed cultural messages that wealth is morally corrupt, that "good people" don't care about money, or that financial success requires compromising your values? These beliefs can create subconscious resistance to improving your financial situation.

The Hidden Costs

The poverty mindset doesn't just affect your bank account—it affects your entire life in ways like the following:

1. **Career Stagnation:** You don't negotiate salaries, ask for promotions, or pursue better opportunities because you don't believe you deserve them.
2. **Relationship Strain:** Constant financial worry creates stress that spills into your relationships. You might decline social invitations, feel embarrassed about your financial situation, or argue with partners about money. Money is the biggest reason for marriages to fail.
3. **Health Impact:** Chronic financial stress releases cortisol, leading to physical health problems, including headaches, sleep issues, digestive problems, and a weakened immune system.
4. **Missed Opportunities:** You pass up investments, education, or business opportunities because you're too focused on protecting what little you have rather than growing it.

Breaking Free from Poverty Mindset

Once you understand what the poverty mindset is, it is helpful to consider whether it is part of how you think.

Step 1: Recognize the Pattern

Start paying attention to your internal dialogue about money. When you think about spending, saving, or earning, what stories do you tell yourself? Write down your thoughts, emotions, and typical behaviors, and take a long look at them. Awareness is the first step to change.

Step 2: Challenge the Thoughts

For each negative thought, ask the following:

- Is this actually true, or is it a feeling disguised as a fact?
- What evidence do I have that contradicts this belief?
- What would I tell a friend who expressed this same fear?

Step 3: Reframe with Truth

Replace scarcity thoughts with abundance thoughts, like the following:

- "There's never enough" becomes "I have enough for today, and I can create opportunities for more."
- "I don't deserve good things" becomes "I have inherent worth regardless of my financial situation."
- "Money will disappear if I'm not careful" becomes "Money is a tool I can learn to manage wisely."

Step 4: Take Small Action Steps

- If you're afraid to spend money on yourself, start with tiny investments in your well-being (five bucks for coffee with a friend, twenty for a book that could help your career).

- If you're afraid to invest, start with twenty-five dollars a month in a simple index fund or your company's retirement plan.
- If you avoid financial opportunities, commit to exploring one small opportunity each month.

The Accumulation Mindset: More Stuff Equals More Happiness

Whether it is print, television, radio, social media influencers, or even our friends and neighbors, advertising encourages us to shop, spend, and buy more. Personal consumption is the biggest part of the national economy. Everything wants us to accept the idea that having more will make us happy. I am here to tell you that it is not true. That is why I have written these books.

What It Looks Like

The accumulation mindset is the belief that acquiring more possessions will bring lasting satisfaction and happiness. It's the internal drive that fills your home with things you rarely use, your garage with storage, and your closets with clothes you never wear.

We always want more.

More money, more achievement, more stuff, more status, more beauty, and so on are what we seek. Do they satisfy us? Do they make us happy? Are our dreams and goals insatiable? According to Arthur C. Brooks, who teaches this at Harvard, satisfaction is the greatest paradox of human life. He found that even though he had accomplished everything on his bucket list, none of that led to lasting joy. This is true for even the most accomplished or successful people.

Our biology seeks homeostasis—bringing us to equilibrium. Our brain also wants to equilibrate our emotions. After a while, the initial boost falls, and we want *more*. It is a treadmill where our satisfaction doesn't last. It takes us nowhere. Money helps—to a point—overcome the problems of poverty. We compare ourselves to others to determine if we are successful or not—keeping up with the Joneses. Is this never-ending seeking a form of idolatry that distracts us from God?

Thomas Aquinas, Buddha (both born into high status), Ralph Waldo Emerson, and Nobel laureates Daniel Kahneman and Amos Tversky all determined that money cannot satisfy us.

What is the alternative—to get off the treadmill?

- *Stop increasing our wants and must-haves.*
- *Focus on intrinsic goals rather than extrinsic goals.*

Consider: What Is Your Motivation for Acquiring More?

> Of course, you want to be rich and famous. It's natural. Wealth and fame are what every man desires. This question is: What are you willing to trade for it?
>
> —Confucius.

Rich people stay rich by living like they are broke. Broke people stay broke by living like they're rich.

—Unknown.

Money and success don't change people; they merely amplify what is already there.

—Will Smith.

Don't think money does everything, or you are going to end up doing everything for money.

—Voltaire.

If you choose money over love, you will always be poor.

—Unknown.

What Is Your Motivation?

Is it for a sense of security?

Is it to pay off debt and be financially free?

Is it to be more generous?

Real-Life Examples

- **TJ, software developer:** He has a good income but lives paycheck to paycheck because every pay increase leads to lifestyle inflation. New salary means new car payment, bigger apartment, and more expensive habits. He owns three gaming systems, a closet full of clothes, and gadgets he's used once.
- **KM, nurse:** She shops when she's stressed, happy, sad, or bored. Her apartment is filled with home décor items, beauty products, and clothes with tags still on them. She estimates she has fifteen thousand

dollars' worth of things she never uses, but she still feels empty and keeps buying more.

- **SS, sales manager:** Every bonus goes to upgrading something—better TV, newer car, fancier watch. He believes these purchases reflect his success, but he's constantly stressed about payments and has no emergency savings despite earning six figures.

The Internal Dialogue

- "This will make me happy."
- "I deserve this after working so hard."
- "Everyone else has one."
- "It's on sale—I'm actually saving money."
- "Once I have [item], I'll be satisfied."
- "This represents my success."

How It Develops

The accumulation mindset is heavily influenced by our consumer culture, which profits from your dissatisfaction. Advertising is designed to make you feel incomplete without the product being sold. Social media amplifies this by constantly showing you what others have, creating artificial needs and desires.

You're especially vulnerable because you're establishing your adult identity. It's natural to want things that represent who you're becoming, but consumer culture exploits this by suggesting your possessions define your worth.

Have you ever heard the expression "retail therapy?" The idea that shopping and spending can solve one of your problems is a sneaky, deceptive lie.

The Psychology Behind It

Accumulation often serves emotional needs rather than practical ones.

- **Identity Expression:** "This reflects who I am."
- **Status Signaling:** "This shows I'm successful."
- **Emotional Regulation:** "Shopping makes me feel better."
- **Control:** "At least I can control what I own."
- **Security:** "Having more means being prepared for anything."

The Hidden Costs

1. **Financial Bondage:** Money that could build wealth gets spent on depreciating assets.
2. **Storage Stress:** You need bigger homes, storage units, and organization systems.
3. **Decision Fatigue:** Too many choices create mental exhaustion.
4. **Maintenance Burden:** Everything you own requires care, cleaning, and eventual replacement.
5. **Opportunity Cost:** Money spent on accumulation can't be used for experiences, generosity, or investments.

The Hedonic Treadmill

Research shows that material purchases provide temporary happiness that fades quickly, leaving you wanting more. This is called the hedonic treadmill. You keep purchasing to maintain the same level of satisfaction, but the baseline keeps shifting higher.

Breaking Free from Accumulation Mindset

Here are steps to consider to regain power over accumulation thinking tendencies.

The Thirty-Day Rule

Before buying anything over fifty dollars, wait thirty days. Write down why you want it and how you expect it to improve your life. Often, the desire fades, revealing it was an impulse rather than a genuine need.

The Joy Audit

Look around your living space. What items genuinely bring you joy when you see or use them? What items do you forget you own? This helps distinguish between meaningful possessions and clutter.

Consider your spending—what parts bring you real joy? If possible, keep select ones, but not too much.

Experience Over Stuff

Research shows experiences create longer-lasting happiness than possessions. Instead of buying things, invest in things like the following:

- Learning new skills

- Traveling (even locally)
- Shared activities with friends
- Hobbies that create rather than consume

The One-In, One-Out Rule

For every new item you bring home, remove one item. This prevents accumulation while forcing you to evaluate whether new purchases are truly worth displacing what you already have.

Redefining Success

Instead of measuring success by possessions, consider measuring it by these metrics:

- Freedom from financial stress
- Ability to be generous
- Time available for relationships and interests
- Progress toward meaningful goals
- Peace of mind about your financial situation

The Comparison Mindset: Keeping Score with Others

We all do it. We cannot help it. If we have eyes to see, we notice when someone in our life (or on TV) changes their hairstyle, buys new clothes or a new car, or moves to a better space. This naturally causes us to compare ourselves and our things with theirs. However, comparison robs you of your joy.

What It Looks Like

The comparison mindset measures your financial success against others, particularly the curated versions you see on social media. You compare your real financial struggles to someone else's financial highlight reel, leaving you feeling inadequate and driving you to spend money to keep up appearances.

Real-Life Examples

- **JR, recent high school graduate:** She goes into credit card debt buying clothes and going to expensive restaurants because her Instagram friends appear to live glamorous lives. She doesn't realize many of them are also in debt or supported by parents.
- **CB, accountant:** He bought a house he couldn't afford because his college friends were all buying homes. Now he's house-poor, stressed about payments, and can't afford to furnish it properly, but at least he can say he's a homeowner.
- **FJ, teacher:** She feels poor because she compares her teacher salary to her friends in tech and finance. This leads her to spend beyond her means trying to keep up with their lifestyle, ignoring the fact that her job provides stability, purpose, and benefits they might envy.

The Internal Dialogue

- "Everyone else can afford this."
- "I should be further along by now."

- "If I don't keep up, people will think I'm unsuccessful."
- "They make it look so easy."
- "I must be doing something wrong."

How Social Media Amplifies Comparison

Social media creates an illusion of transparency while actually showing you carefully curated financial highlights like the following:

- Vacation photos don't show credit card debt.
- New car posts don't mention the monthly payment stress.
- Restaurant photos don't reveal the empty savings account.
- Career announcements don't mention the anxiety and long hours.

Seeing others prosper while you struggle can create confusion and resentment. Remember that each person is unique, and financial circumstances don't reflect your worth.

The Relativity Trap

Your sense of wealth is relative to your reference group. Someone making fifty grand might feel wealthy compared to college friends still in entry-level jobs, but poor compared to friends in high-paying careers. The same person can feel rich or poor depending on who they're comparing themselves to.

Breaking Free from Comparison Mindset

Now that we have discussed the problems with comparison thinking, what can we do about it?

Curate Your Inputs

- Unfollow social media accounts that consistently make you feel inadequate.
- Follow accounts that inspire without intimidating.
- Limit time on social media platforms that trigger comparison.
- Remember that social media is advertising, not reality.

Focus on Your Own Growth

Instead of comparing your current situation to others, compare it to your past self.

- Are you making better financial decisions than last year?
- Have you learned new money management skills?
- Are you closer to your personal goals?
- Do you have more peace about money than before?

Practice Gratitude

When you catch yourself comparing, immediately shift to gratitude.

- List three things you're financially grateful for.

- Remember the advantages you have that others might envy.
- Focus on nonfinancial blessings in your life.

Get the Full Story

When you're tempted to compare, remember you're seeing a tiny slice of someone's full reality.

- The successful-looking friend might have massive student loans.
- The person with the nice car might be living with parents to afford it.
- The frequent traveler might be neglecting retirement savings.
- The designer outfit might have been bought on credit.

How These Mindsets Work Together

These three mindsets often combine to create a perfect storm of financial dysfunction. You might simultaneously believe you don't have enough (poverty), need to acquire more to be happy (accumulation), and must keep up with others to maintain your status (comparison).

Example: The Debt Spiral

SM has a poverty mindset that makes her fear spending money on herself, but she also has comparison issues that drive her to keep up appearances. She'll skip buying lunch to save twelve dollars, but then spend two hundred on an outfit for a party because she can't bear to look "cheap" in front of friends. The accumulation mindset kicks in as she convinces herself she "deserves" the outfit, and it will make her feel confident. The result? She's simultaneously depriving herself of basic needs and overspending on status symbols.

The Roots of Destructive Mindsets

Understanding where these mindsets come from helps you address them more effectively. Here are roots of these mindsets.

Childhood Experiences

- Growing up in financial stress creates anxiety around money.
- Parents who argue about money teach that money causes conflict.
- Being told "we can't afford that" repeatedly creates scarcity beliefs.
- Seeing money used for control or manipulation affects trust.
- Having basic needs unmet creates hoarding tendencies.

Cultural Messages

- "You deserve the best" encourages entitlement.
- "Success means having nice things" ties identity to possessions.
- "Everyone else is doing better" promotes comparison.

- "Money isn't important" creates guilt about financial goals.
- "Rich people are greedy" creates resistance to wealth building.

Traumatic Experiences

- Job loss, foreclosure, or bankruptcy creates lasting fear.
- Financial betrayal by trusted people affects money relationships.
- Sudden windfalls followed by loss create boom-bust patterns.
- Economic recessions during formative years affect risk tolerance.

Social Environment

- Peer groups that overspend create pressure to keep up.
- Social media creates unrealistic comparison standards.
- Dating culture that expects expensive activities strains budgets.
- Career environments that emphasize status symbols can encourage overspending.

Develop Healthy Money Mindsets

Changing your mindset isn't about positive thinking or denying reality—it's about seeing your financial situation clearly and responding wisely rather than emotionally.

The Abundance Mindset

Instead of the poverty mindset, I suggest the abundance mindset, which is discussed next.

Core Belief: There are enough resources and opportunities for everyone to succeed.

Characteristics

- Grateful for current blessings while working toward goals
- Generous with others because you believe there's enough to share
- Willing to invest in growth because you expect positive returns
- Collaborative rather than competitive in approach
- Focused on creating value rather than just acquiring resources

Applications

- You celebrate others' success instead of feeling threatened.
- You invest in education and skills because you believe in future opportunities.

- You're willing to spend money on things that align with your values.
- You can be generous even when your income is modest.
- You make financial decisions based on wisdom rather than fear.

The Stewardship Mindset

The resources that we have are like gifts that have been given to us. Even when we earn a paycheck, it is because we have been given the ability to learn, work, and earn. So what should we do with these things that we have, blessings that have been entrusted to us?

Core Belief: Money is a tool to be managed wisely for good purposes.

This is being a faithful steward of resources. Your money isn't ultimately yours—you're managing for a higher purpose.

This means viewing money as a responsibility rather than just a right. You have an obligation to use financial resources thoughtfully, considering the impact on yourself, your family, and society.

Characteristics

- Considerate of how other people and the planet are affected by your money decisions
- Careful with money but not anxious about it
- Generous without being foolish

- Future-focused without neglecting present needs
- Accountable to values and principles rather than just desires
- Sees money as having moral and social dimensions

The Growth Mindset

I like to think that I learn something every day. There are endless ways to improve myself. I've heard it said that we are either growing or dying. SMART (Specific, Measurable, Achievable, Relevant, and Time-based) Goals are ways to grow.

Core Belief: Financial skills and situations can improve through learning and effort.

Characteristics

- Plans for the future
- Views financial mistakes as learning opportunities
- Believes the ability to manage money can be developed
- Seeks education and advice to improve
- Takes calculated risks for gain
- Focuses on process and progress rather than just outcomes

Exercises for Mindset Change

Here are practical steps to help you actually change how you think—your mindset.

The Mindset Journal

For one week, track your thoughts about money throughout the day.

- What triggers financial anxiety or excitement?
- What stories do you tell yourself about purchases?
- How do you feel before, during, and after spending money?
- What financial thoughts distract you from other activities?

Look for patterns. Are your thoughts mostly focused on scarcity or abundance? Do you spend time worrying about things outside your control?

The Gratitude Inventory

A gratitude inventory is a list of everything you are grateful for.

Make three lists.

1. **Financial blessings:** Income sources, possessions that add genuine value, people who've helped you financially, opportunities you've had.
2. **Nonfinancial blessings:** Relationships, health, skills, experiences, natural beauty, freedoms you enjoy.

3. **Lessons learned:** Financial mistakes that taught valuable lessons, challenges that built character, setbacks that led to better outcomes.

Review these lists when comparison or scarcity thinking creeps in.

The Values Alignment Check

Check in with yourself and objectively evaluate what you think about. Remember, we are what we think about.

1. **Identify your top five values** (examples: family, creativity, security, adventure, service, learning, freedom, sustainability).
2. **Review your last month's spending** and categorize each expense.
3. **Calculate what percentage** of your spending aligned with each value.
4. **Ask yourself,** "Does my spending reflect what I say matters most to me?"

This exercise often reveals disconnects between stated values and actual financial behavior.

See Your Future Self

Imagine yourself ten years from now, having successfully developed healthy money mindsets.

- How do you make financial decisions?
- What does your relationship with money look like?
- How do you feel when you spend, save, and earn?

- What financial habits have become automatic?
- How has this transformation affected other areas of your life?

Write this vision down and refer to it when you need motivation to change current patterns.

Overcome Common Obstacles

You are not alone. There are very common obstacles that we all face throughout our lives. Here are strategies to overcome them.

"But I Really Don't Have Enough."

Sometimes scarcity isn't just a mindset—it's a reality. If you're truly struggling to meet basic needs, the goal isn't to pretend everything is fine. Instead, try the following:

1. **Separate temporary circumstances from permanent identity:** "I'm currently in a tight financial situation" is different from "I'm a poor person."
2. **Focus on what you can control:** Even in difficult circumstances, you have choices about how to respond.
3. **Look for small opportunities:** Can you earn extra income? Reduce any expenses? Learn skills that might help long-term?
4. **Seek appropriate help:** There's no shame in using community resources, government assistance, or help from family and friends when genuinely needed.

"Positive Thinking Feels Fake."

Mindset change isn't about forcing fake optimism. It's about these concepts.

1. **Accuracy over positivity:** See your situation clearly rather than through the lens of fear or wishful thinking.
2. **Agency over attitude:** Focus on what actions you can take rather than just trying to feel better.
3. **Process over outcomes:** Celebrate good financial decisions regardless of immediate results.
4. **Growth over perfection:** Progress matters more than having everything figured out.

"My Family/Friends Don't Support This."

Changing your money mindset might create tension with people who prefer you stay the same.

1. **Expect resistance:** People often feel threatened when others change, even positively.
2. **Set boundaries:** You don't need everyone's approval to improve your financial life.
3. **Find support elsewhere:** Seek friends, mentors, or communities that encourage growth.
4. **Be patient:** Sometimes people need time to adjust to your changes.

The Ripple Effects of Mindset Change

When you shift from destructive to healthy money mindsets, the effects extend far beyond your bank account.

Relationships Improve: Less financial stress means less tension with family and friends. You can be more generous and present because you're not constantly worried about money.

Career Advances: Abundance thinking leads to better negotiations, a willingness to take calculated risks, and investment in skill development.

Health Benefits: Reduced financial anxiety decreases stress hormones, improving sleep, immunity, and overall physical health.

Spiritual Growth: Proper money mindsets can deepen faith and trust in God. For others, it can clarify values and increase sense of purpose.

Generosity Increases: When you move from scarcity to abundance thinking, you naturally become more generous with time, money, and attention.

Decision Quality Improves: Rational decisions, rather than fear-based ones, typically lead to better long-term outcomes.

Move Forward

Remember, mindset change is a process, not an event. You'll likely still experience moments of scarcity thinking, comparison, or accumulation desire. The goal isn't perfection—it's progress toward financial thoughts and behaviors that serve your long-term well-being.

Start with awareness. Notice your financial thoughts and emotions without immediately trying to change them. Understanding your current patterns is the first step toward developing new ones.

Then, begin making small shifts. Replace one scarcity thought with an abundance thought. Choose one purchase based on values rather than comparison. Practice gratitude for one financial blessing each day. How does this make you feel?

These small changes compound over time, eventually transforming not just how you think about money, but how you experience life itself. The mindset trap that currently limits your financial potential can become the foundation for financial freedom, generosity, and peace.

Conclusion Chapter Two

Your current financial struggles may have less to do with your income level than with your money mindset. Consider these common but destructive thought patterns.

The Poverty Mindset keeps you focused on what you don't have, convincing you that there will never be enough. This scarcity thinking creates a cycle of worry, fear, and sometimes self-sabotage. You may think that you deserve to be impoverished. You might find yourself saying things like "I can't afford that" even when you can, or avoiding opportunities because you're afraid of financial risk. The poverty mindset is particularly cruel because it often becomes a self-fulfilling prophecy—when you believe you'll always struggle financially, you make decisions that ensure you will.

- *A poverty mindset can lead to short-term thinking, rather than delaying gratification and having a better result for the rest of your life—lasting gratification.*
- *Rich people think differently about money than poor people do.*
- *My grandparents grew up in the Great Depression. Baby boomers (as a group) had unprecedented wealth compared to their predecessors. Gen X and Gen Z will have different life experiences and situations, which impact how they think about money.*
- *The "Good Old Days" weren't good for everyone. Some families are living with generational poverty. This is because if your parents or grandparents lacked financial security, it is more likely that you will too.*
- *Retired people are told to fear "outliving their money (savings)."*

The Accumulation Mindset drives you to believe that more stuff equals more happiness. This shows up in the constant desire for bigger homes, newer cars, and the latest gadgets. You might find your home filling up with possessions you rarely use, your garage becoming a storage unit, or your closets overflowing with clothes you never wear. The accumulation mindset promises satisfaction but delivers only temporary pleasure followed by the need for more.

- *I know people whose only goal is to have as much money as possible. Love and life purpose aren't their concerns.*
- *Do you make decisions about money—without considering the purpose of your life?*
- *Don't buy something you cannot afford to lose. It is just as easy to lose a five-hundred-dollar pair of sunglasses as it is a thirty dollar pair of sunglasses.*
- *If you own something that you cannot give away, it owns you.*

—Albert Schweitzer

The Comparison Mindset is about pride, which keeps you measuring your financial success against others, particularly the curated versions of others you see on social media. You compare your real financial struggles to someone else's financial highlight reel, leaving you feeling inadequate and driving you to spend money to keep up appearances. This mindset is especially dangerous in our digital age, where influencers and advertising constantly show us idealized versions of lifestyle and success.

- *Do you compare yourself to the Instagram or TikTok version of someone else? Remember that these are highly stylized, like a movie set, and not realistic. Do you think you need to spend money on name-brand shoes or other products?*

- *Do you compare your home to the HGTV renovated homes and decide that you need to spend money as a result?*
- *Do you own your big house? Or does your house own you?*

These mindsets often work together, creating a perfect storm of financial dysfunction. You might simultaneously believe you don't have enough (poverty), need to acquire more to be happy (accumulation), and must keep up with others to maintain your status (comparison).

In the next chapter, we'll explore the specific stories you tell yourself that either support or undermine these healthy mindsets. Because changing how you think about money requires changing the narratives that run in the background of your financial decisions.

CHAPTER 3

The Stories We Tell Ourselves

> The stories we tell ourselves about our capabilities and about the meaning of our own experience guide our actions and shape our reality.
>
> —Brené Brown

The Power of Internal Narratives

Before you make any financial decision—whether it's buying a coffee, signing a lease, or choosing a career—your mind creates a story to justify that choice. These internal narratives happen so quickly and automatically that you're rarely aware of them, yet they're more powerful than logic, budgets, or even desperate circumstances in determining your financial behavior.

Think about the last time you made a purchase you later regretted. What did you tell yourself in the moment to justify it? What story made that spending both feel acceptable and necessary? Understanding these internal narratives is crucial because they reveal the deeper beliefs and fears that drive your financial decisions.

See it: Imagine your mind as a movie director, constantly creating short films to explain your financial choices. Each purchase, each financial goal, each money decision gets its own mini-movie with characters, plot, and emotional soundtrack. These stories feel so real that you experience them as truth rather than narrative.

Feel it: Think of these stories as the fuel in your financial engine. Just as a car needs gas to run, your financial decisions need internal narratives to feel justified. Different stories create different kinds of energy—some stories fuel wise decisions, others power destructive choices.

Hear it: Consider these internal narratives as the voice-over narration of your financial life. Like a documentary where the narrator explains what's happening and why it matters, your internal voice constantly provides commentary that shapes how you interpret and respond to financial situations.

Why We Create Financial Stories

Human beings are meaning-making creatures. We can't just act—we need reasons, justifications, and narratives that help us feel our choices make sense. This is especially true with money because financial decisions often involve conflict between what we want now and what's good for us long-term, between what we can afford and what we desire, between our values and our impulses.

These stories serve several psychological functions.

Identity Protection: They help maintain your self-image as a good, smart, deserving person even when making questionable financial choices.

Anxiety Reduction: They provide certainty and control in uncertain financial situations.

Social Justification: They give you explanations for financial choices that others might question.

Motivation Creation: They generate emotional energy to take action, even when logic alone wouldn't be compelling enough.

The problem is that while these stories feel helpful in the moment, many of them actually work against your long-term financial well-being. They're like sugar—they provide quick emotional energy but create bigger problems over time.

The Most Destructive Financial Stories

Let's examine the most common and dangerous stories people tell themselves, along with the real-world consequences and healthier alternatives.

Story #1: "I Deserve This."

What It Sounds Like

- "I've had a rough week—I deserve this expensive dinner."
- "I work so hard, I deserve nice things."
- "After everything I've been through, I deserve some happiness."
- "I've been so good with money lately, I deserve a splurge."
- "Life is short, and I deserve to enjoy it."

The Psychology Behind It

This story appeals to your sense of fairness and self-worth. It suggests that your suffering, effort, or virtue has earned you the right to spend money you don't have or shouldn't spend. It transforms financial irresponsibility into moral justice.

Real-Life Examples

Years ago, I lived and worked in the Los Angeles area and traveled to Southeast Asia for work. The day before I left for the trip, my husband and I moved into the ugliest fixer-upper house that I was embarrassed to even own—it was the only thing I could afford. After all of my schooling, diligent effort, and career advancement, surely, I deserved something better. Then I got off the plane in Bangkok. During the drive from the airport to the hotel, I changed my mind completely. My mind was blown to see how the people lived. They lived next to open sewers, with a piece of sheet metal leaning on a rickety wooden structure. I needed to change my perspective. I needed to repent. Those people were the ones I should think about.

I know people who expect and feel they deserve to have a dream home and fabulous vacations. They don't know that having a middle-class lifestyle is a relatively new possibility for people in history. They don't even have a thought or care about others who will never have such a thing. They don't know about people experiencing generational poverty, extreme poverty, or being forcibly displaced from their homes. They may not realize that many people don't have access to sanitation, safe drinking water, or an adequate education. They may not know that some families in the world sell their daughters (sons, too, but mostly girls) to support the rest of the family. They may not think about how our lifestyle affects others, as well as the earth we live on, the plants, animals, air, water, biodiversity, and sustainability. And yet, they feel deprived.

Many years ago, I knew a woman who was a CPA with a large CPA firm leading the audit of the financial statements for the company where I worked. During the time we were working together, she purchased a full set of living room furniture. She made the statement that she "deserved it."

I thought about this statement. I did not disagree with her that she had worked hard to become a CPA and continued to work hard in the demanding career.

I also thought about other people who work just as hard. Most others did not have the same opportunities that she or I had. It may be parents with young children, working two or three jobs to keep a roof over their heads and food on the table (presuming they have a table). It may be people with serious medical issues in their families. It may be people who did not live in safe homes growing up. Their parents may not have had stable employment. They may not have lived where there were good public schools. They may live in a country or neighborhood that has dealt with armed conflict. They may have lived in communities with little opportunity or few role models for how to have a better life. They may have had addiction in their families. The list goes on and on. Although others' circumstances may have been different, they were no less deserving if they worked hard.

I realized, it isn't about who "deserves it." It is about our mindset, how we think, especially about our self-worth, our priorities (like generosity), and our expectations. It is about whether or not we are willing to delay gratification (for lasting gratification), whether or not we compare ourselves to others, and who those others are.

JM works as a nurse in a busy hospital. After a particularly difficult shift where she lost a patient, she goes to an expensive spa and charges three hundred dollars to her credit card for treatments she can't afford. Her internal story is, "After what I went through today, I deserve to be pampered. My emotional well-being is worth more than money."

While JM's desire for comfort after trauma is understandable and her work is genuinely valuable, the "I deserve this" story led her to make a financial choice that will create additional stress through debt. Her emotional pain was real, but the story that expensive pampering was the solution was destructive.

Why This Story Is Dangerous

1. **It confuses deserving with affording:** Deserving something and being able to afford it are completely different things.
2. **It creates an endless cycle:** There will always be new reasons why you "deserve" something.
3. **It uses emotions to override rational financial planning:** Present emotions become more important than future consequences.
4. **It assumes that spending money is the primary way to address nonfinancial problems:** Stress, sadness, and difficulty rarely require financial solutions.

Cultural Reinforcement

Our consumer culture actively promotes this story through advertising.

- "You deserve a break today." (McDonald's)
- "Because you're worth it." (L'Oréal)

- "Treat yourself." (countless brands)
- "You work hard—you should play hard."

These messages aren't just selling products—they're selling a story about worthiness that connects your self-esteem to your spending.

The Hidden Costs

Using "I deserve this" as a financial justification creates several problems.

- **Debt accumulation** from purchases you can't afford.
- **Guilt cycles** where splurging leads to shame, which leads to more "deserve" spending to feel better.
- **Delayed financial goals** because "deserving" purchases take priority over saving.
- **Identity confusion** where your worth becomes tied to what you buy rather than who you are.

Healthier Alternatives

Instead of "I deserve this expensive thing," try the following:

- "I deserve to make wise choices that support my long-term well-being."
- "I deserve to find ways to celebrate/comfort myself that don't harm my financial future."
- "I deserve to address the real issue behind this desire, not just medicate it with spending."
- "I deserve to have financial peace more than I deserve this purchase."

Applications

When you catch yourself using the "deserve" story, try these techniques.

1. **Pause and identify the underlying need:** Are you tired? Stressed? Celebrating? Grieving? Address the actual need rather than medicating it with spending.
2. **Separate worth from spending:** Your value as a person is not dependent on what you own or how much you spend on yourself.
3. **Find nonfinancial ways to honor your worth:** Take a bath, call a friend, go for a walk, journal, listen to music—many forms of self-care cost little or nothing.
4. **Reframe "deserving":** You deserve financial peace, security, and freedom more than you deserve any specific purchase.

Story #2: "I'll Pay for It Somehow."

What It Sounds Like

- "I really need this now. I'll figure out the payment later."
- "Something will work out."
- "I might get a bonus/tax refund/gift that will cover it."
- "I can always put it on a credit card."
- "Future me will have more money."
- "I'll just work extra hours to pay for it."

The Psychology Behind It

This story is magical thinking disguised as optimism. It allows you to make purchases without a realistic plan for payment by assuming that future circumstances will somehow solve present financial decisions. It treats money as if it will materialize through hope rather than planning.

Real-Life Examples

KK sees a deal on a used motorcycle for four thousand dollars. He has five hundred in savings and already lives paycheck to paycheck, but he tells himself, "This is such a good deal, I can't pass it up. I'll figure out how to pay for it. Maybe I can get overtime at work, or my tax refund might be bigger than expected."

KK purchases the motorcycle using a personal loan with high interest rates. When the overtime doesn't materialize, and his tax refund is smaller than he had hoped, he struggles with payments. His credit score drops, and he eventually has to sell the motorcycle at a loss.

LA books a two-thousand-dollar vacation with friends using her credit card despite having no savings. Her story is, "I work so hard, I need this vacation. Plus, all my friends are going—I can't miss out. I'll pick up extra shifts when I get back to pay for it."

When LA returns from vacation, she's exhausted and unable to work extra shifts. The vacation debt takes eight months to pay off, costing an additional three hundred dollars in interest charges and preventing her from saving for other goals.

Why This Story Is Dangerous

1. **It robs you of your future:** You will have less money each month in the future and fewer options.
2. **It treats future income as guaranteed:** Life is unpredictable—illness, job changes, or other expenses can disrupt income plans.
3. **It ignores opportunity cost:** Money used to pay for impulsive purchases can't be used for planned goals.
4. **It creates debt cycles:** When the "somehow" doesn't materialize, credit becomes the solution, leading to compound problems.
5. **It prevents realistic financial planning:** If you assume money will "work out," you don't develop actual financial strategies.

The Magical Thinking Problem

This story assumes that wanting something badly enough will somehow create the resources to afford it. It's the financial equivalent of believing that if you jump off a building and flap your arms hard enough, you'll be able to fly.

Hidden Psychological Functions

The "I'll pay for it somehow" story often masks several things.

- **Present bias:** Overvaluing immediate pleasure compared to future consequences.

- **Anxiety about decision-making:** Making the purchase eliminates the stress of deciding whether to buy it.
- **Control illusions:** Believing you have more control over future circumstances than you actually do.
- **Fear of missing out (FOMO):** "If I don't buy this now, I'll never get another chance." This fear might drive you to spend money on experiences you can't afford because everyone else is doing them, invest in trendy assets (like cryptocurrency or meme stocks) without understanding their risks, upgrade your lifestyle beyond your means to keep up with peers, or even take on debt for travel, dining, or entertainment to avoid feeling left out.

Healthier Alternatives

Replace "I'll figure it out" with other alternatives.

- "If I can't afford it now with cash, I can't afford it."
- "Let me create a specific savings plan for this purchase."
- "If this is truly important, I can wait and budget for it properly."
- "I'll revisit this purchase when I have a concrete payment plan."

Applications

1. **The Forty-Eight-Hour Rule:** When tempted to make an unplanned purchase, wait forty-eight hours and

develop a specific payment plan. If you can't create a realistic plan, don't make the purchase.

2. **Future Income Reality Check:** Assume your income will stay the same or potentially decrease. Don't spend money based on hoped-for income increases.
3. **Emergency Fund Protection:** Never assume you can use emergency funds for non-emergencies, even temporarily.
4. **Payment Plan Requirement:** Before any significant purchase, write down exactly where every dollar will come from. Vague plans like "work more" or "cut expenses somewhere" don't count.

Story #3: "Everyone Else Has One."

What It Sounds Like

- "All my friends have the latest iPhone."
- "Everyone in my office has a nice car."
- "Normal people my age live in apartments like this."
- "I can't be the only one without [item]."
- "This is just what people in my position are expected to have."
- "I'm behind compared to my peers."

The Psychology Behind It

This story transforms spending into social survival. It suggests that financial decisions aren't really about money—they're about belonging, acceptance, and avoiding social rejection. It makes purchases feel mandatory rather than optional.

Real-Life Examples

BN works in tech and feels pressure to have expensive gadgets, designer clothing, and frequent expensive meals with colleagues. His story is, "In my industry, image matters. If I look cheap, people won't take me seriously. Everyone else can afford this stuff, so I should be able to as well."

BN accumulates twenty thousand dollars in credit card debt trying to maintain an image that he believes is professionally necessary. He doesn't realize that many of his colleagues either earn significantly more than he does, have family financial support, or are also in debt maintaining their lifestyle.

ST moves to an expensive apartment because her college friends all live in similar places. Her story is, "I can't be the only one still living like a student. Everyone else has figured out how to afford nice places—there must be something wrong with my financial situation."

ST doesn't know that some friends have family help with rent, others have roommates, and some are stretching their budgets to dangerous levels. Her assumption that "everyone else" can easily afford their lifestyle leads her to make housing choices that consume 60 percent of her income.

Why This Story Is Dangerous

1. **It uses comparison thinking:** You compare yourself to others.

2. **It's based on incomplete information:** You see others' purchases but not their full financial picture—their debt, family support, different income levels, or financial stress.
3. **It assumes uniform circumstances:** "Everyone else" likely has different financial situations, priorities, and resources than you do.
4. **It makes spending feel mandatory:** You lose the sense that you have choices about how to spend your money.
5. **It creates artificial urgency:** Fear of being left out drives immediate purchasing rather than thoughtful planning.

The Social Media Amplification

Social media makes this story particularly destructive.

- **Curated highlights:** You see everyone's best purchases and experiences, not their financial struggles.
- **False abundance:** The constant stream of others' lifestyle photos creates the illusion that luxury is normal.
- **FOMO intensification:** Fear of missing out becomes constant rather than occasional.
- **Comparison amplification:** You compare yourself not just to close friends but to hundreds of acquaintances and influencers.

The Peer Pressure Evolution

Adult peer pressure around money is often more subtle but more expensive than teenage peer pressure.

- **Professional pressure:** "Dressing for success" and networking expenses.
- **Social pressure:** Keeping up with friends' lifestyle inflation.
- **Dating pressure:** Expensive restaurants, activities, and appearance expectations.
- **Family pressure:** Living up to relatives' expectations or achievements.

Cultural Context

Different communities have different "normal" spending patterns.

- **Geographic differences:** What seems necessary in Manhattan might be a luxury in rural areas.
- **Industry differences:** Tech workers, lawyers, and teachers have different professional spending norms.
- **Generational differences:** Different age groups have different expectations about lifestyle timing.

Healthier Alternatives

Replace "everyone else has one" with these alternatives.

- "I don't know everyone else's full financial situation."
- "My financial decisions should be based on my circumstances and goals, not others' choices."

- "I can choose to be different if it serves my long-term well-being."
- "True friends will accept me regardless of what I own."

Applications

1. **Realistically check your assumptions:** Ask yourself what evidence you actually have about others' financial situations. Usually, it's much less than you think.
2. **Broaden your reference group:** Instead of just comparing yourself to big spenders, notice people who live more simply and seem content.
3. **Values-based decisions:** Before purchases, ask whether they align with your values and goals, not whether they match others' choices.
4. **Conversation starters:** Consider having honest conversations with trusted friends about money. You might discover they share your financial concerns.

Story #4: "I Can't Change My Situation."

What It Sounds Like

- "I'll never make enough money."
- "I'll always struggle with debt."
- "Financial success is for other people, not me."
- "I'm just not good with money."
- "My circumstances are too difficult to overcome."
- "I don't have the advantages other people have."

The Psychology Behind It

This story protects you from the risk and effort required for financial change by making that change seem impossible. If your situation truly can't improve, then you're not responsible for improving it, and you don't have to face the discomfort of trying new approaches or potentially failing.

Real-Life Examples

AR has been living paycheck to paycheck for years despite having a decent income as a teacher. Her story is, "Teachers just don't make enough money to get ahead. The system is rigged against people like me. I could never afford to invest or save significantly—that's for people who make six figures."

AR's story prevents her from exploring budgeting strategies, side income opportunities, or investment options appropriate for her income level. She doesn't realize that many teachers successfully build wealth through careful financial planning, and that her income, while modest, could support some savings and investing.

JL grew up in poverty and now earns a middle-class income but still struggles financially. His story is, "I never learned how to manage money growing up. Rich people just know things I don't know. I'm destined to struggle because of where I came from."

JL's story prevents him from seeking financial education, advice, or trying new money management strategies. He doesn't recognize that financial literacy can be learned at any age and that his background, while challenging, doesn't determine his future.

Why This Story Is Dangerous

1. **It becomes self-fulfilling:** If you believe change is impossible, you won't try strategies that could actually work.
2. **It prevents learning:** Why seek financial education if you believe you're incapable of improvement?
3. **It creates a victim mentality:** External circumstances become more powerful than your choices and actions.
4. **It ignores gradual progress:** Small improvements compound over time, but this story dismisses them as meaningless.

The Learned Helplessness Problem

Psychologist Martin Seligman's research on learned helplessness shows that when people repeatedly experience uncontrollable negative events, they often generalize that helplessness to situations where they actually do have control. Past financial setbacks can create this pattern with money.

Common Variations

This story manifests differently for different people.

For Those from Low-Income Backgrounds

- "Money is for rich people."
- "I don't deserve wealth."
- "Financial success means forgetting where I came from."

For Those Who've Made Financial Mistakes

- "I've already ruined my finances."
- "I'm too old to start over."
- "My credit is destroyed forever."

For Those Facing Current Challenges

- "My income is too low to make a difference."
- "I have too much debt to ever get ahead."
- "My expenses are too high to save anything."

Healthier Alternatives

Replace "I can't change" with these alternatives.

- "I may not be able to change everything, but I can change some things."
- "Small improvements compound over time."
- "I can learn new financial skills at any age."
- "My past doesn't determine my future."
- "Even modest progress is valuable."

Applications

1. **Start with tiny changes:** Success with small financial improvements builds confidence for larger changes.
2. **Seek education:** Read books, take courses, or find mentors who can teach you meaningful financial strategies.

3. **Focus on what you can control:** You may not control your salary, but you can control your spending patterns, learning habits, and financial goals.
4. **Celebrate progress:** Acknowledge improvements even if they feel small—they're building momentum for larger changes.

Story #5: "This Will Make Me Happy."

What It Sounds Like

- "Once I have this, I'll finally be satisfied."
- "This purchase will solve my problem."
- "I'll feel so much better if I buy this."
- "This is exactly what's missing from my life."
- "I'll be more confident/attractive/successful with this."

The Psychology Behind It

This story promises that external purchases can fix internal problems. It treats money as emotional medicine and possessions as happiness delivery systems. It assumes that the right purchase will create lasting positive feelings.

Why This Story Appeals to Us

- **Immediate gratification:** Shopping provides instant dopamine hits.
- **Control illusion:** Purchasing feels like taking action to improve your life.
- **Identity expression:** Products seem to represent who we want to become.

- **Problem avoidance:** Buying things is easier than addressing underlying issues.

The Hedonic Treadmill Reality

Research consistently shows that material purchases provide temporary happiness that fades quickly, leaving you at the same baseline emotional state but with less money. This creates a cycle where you need increasingly frequent or expensive purchases to maintain the same level of temporary satisfaction.

Healthier Alternatives

Before making purchases for emotional reasons, try these alternatives.

1. **Identify the real need:** Are you lonely? Stressed? Bored? Insecure? Address the actual issue rather than medicating it with spending.
2. **Try nonfinancial solutions first:** Exercising, socializing, creating, learning, or serving others often address the underlying need more effectively than purchasing.
3. **Wait twenty-four hours:** Let the emotional intensity pass before making the purchase.
4. **Consider experiences over objects:** Research shows experiences create longer-lasting happiness than possessions.

Create Healthier Financial Stories

Once you recognize your destructive financial stories, you can begin creating healthier narratives that support your long-term well-being.

Characteristics of Healthy Financial Stories

Realistic: They acknowledge both opportunities and constraints in your situation.

Empowering: They focus on what you can control rather than what you can't.

Values-based: They align with your deeper principles and long-term goals.

Growth-oriented: They assume you can learn and improve over time.

Present-focused: They help you make good decisions now rather than dwelling on past mistakes or future fantasies.

Examples of Healthy Financial Stories

- Instead of "I deserve this expensive thing," try "I deserve to make choices that support my long-term happiness and security."
- Instead of "I'll figure out how to pay for it," try "If I can't afford it now, I'll create a savings plan to afford it later."

- Instead of "Everyone else has one," try "I make financial decisions based on my own values and circumstances, not others' choices."
- Instead of "I can't change my situation," try "I may not be able to change everything immediately, but I can make progress over time."
- Instead of "This will make me happy," try "I'll address my emotional needs directly rather than hoping purchases will fix them."

The Story Transformation Process

Changing your financial stories isn't about positive thinking or denial—it's about developing more accurate and empowering narratives.

Step 1: Recognition

Start noticing the stories you tell yourself about money. You can do this by using these tactics.

- Keep a journal of thoughts that precede financial decisions.
- Pay attention to the language you use when talking about money.
- Consider your emotional responses.
- Notice patterns in your financial justifications.
- Ask yourself, "What story am I telling myself right now?"

Step 2: Examination

For each story, ask the following:

- Is this story actually true, or does it just feel true?
- What evidence supports or contradicts this narrative?
- How is this story serving me? How is it limiting me?
- Where did this story come from (childhood, culture, past experiences)?
- What would I tell a friend who expressed this same story?

Step 3: Rewriting

Create alternative stories that are the following:

- More accurate to your actual situation
- Focused on what you can control
- Aligned with your values and goals
- Empowering rather than limiting
- Supportive of long-term well-being

Step 4: Practice

- Catch yourself when old stories arise and consciously replace them.
- Write down new stories and review them regularly.
- Share healthier stories with trusted friends for accountability.
- Celebrate when you make decisions based on better narratives.

Step 5: Patience

Changing internal narratives takes time. Be patient with yourself as you develop new patterns of thinking about money.

Special Considerations for Different Groups

Faith-Based Wisdom

Financial principles can provide powerful alternative stories.

- "I'm a steward of God's resources" instead of "This is my money to do with as I please."
- "God will provide for my needs" instead of "I must hoard money to feel secure."
- "Contentment is great gain" instead of "More stuff will make me happy."
- "Give, and it will be given to you" instead of "I can only be generous with leftovers."

However, be careful not to use faith as an excuse for poor financial planning ("God will provide" shouldn't justify financial irresponsibility) or to create shame about legitimate financial needs and goals.

Wisdom

You can create meaningful financial stories based on the following:

- **Personal values:** "I spend money in ways that reflect what matters most to me."
- **Future self:** "I make decisions that my future self will thank me for."
- **Community impact:** "My financial choices affect not just me but others around me."
- **Legacy thinking:** "I want to use money in ways I'll be proud of."

For Those from Low-Income Backgrounds

You might need to specifically counter stories that equate wealth with moral corruption or that suggest financial success means abandoning your roots.

- "I can build wealth while maintaining my values and relationships."
- "Financial security helps me serve others better."
- "I can honor where I came from while creating a different financial future."

For Those with Past Financial Trauma

If bankruptcy, foreclosure, job loss, or other financial trauma created lasting stories about money, try to center these thoughts.

- "Past financial setbacks were learning experiences, not permanent failures."
- "I can rebuild financial security gradually and sustainably."

- "One financial crisis doesn't define my entire financial future."

The Ripple Effects of Story Change

When you change your financial stories, the effects extend beyond money.

Improved Decision-Making: Better stories lead to better choices in all areas of life.

Reduced Anxiety: Accurate, empowering stories create less stress than fearful, limiting ones.

Better Relationships: Healthier money stories often improve relationships by reducing financial stress and conflict.

Increased Confidence: Success with financial story change builds confidence for other personal development.

Greater Authenticity: Living according to your values rather than unconscious stories feels more genuine.

Move Forward: Your New Financial Narrative

The stories you tell yourself about money either support or undermine every financial decision you make. By becoming aware of your current narratives and consciously choosing healthier ones, you take control of one of the most powerful forces shaping your financial life.

Remember, you're not trying to eliminate all financial stories—you're upgrading them to serve your well-being rather than work against it. The goal is stories that are true, empowering, and aligned with your deepest values and long-term goals.

Conclusion Chapter Three

Every financial decision you make is preceded by a story you tell yourself about what that decision means. These internal narratives are often more powerful than the reality of your financial situation. Here are the most common and destructive financial stories.

"I deserve this." This story justifies spending you can't afford by appealing to your sense of fairness or reward. After a hard week at work, you "deserve" an expensive dinner. After dealing with stress, you "deserve" a shopping trip. The problem is that deserving something and being able to afford it are two entirely different things.

There is no such thing as a self-made man or woman. Some financially successful people seem to think that they did it on their own. However, they may not fully appreciate the blessings of their life situation as compared with others. Examples could include generational poverty, residing in a war-torn society, not having access to good education, good jobs, or the obstacle of discrimination in the forms of race, sex, ethnicity, culture, or social class. There is considerable evidence that there is not a "level playing field." Does this mean that they did not take advantage of opportunities? Did they have bootstraps with which to pull themselves up? Should we "look down" on them? Not all people have bootstraps to pull themselves up by. Business owners benefited from having employees educated in public schools, having security of public-financed law enforcement and military, roads, sewers, airports, and seaports paid by public money.

- *In America, we think individualistically as opposed to communally.*
- *When you see people who are less well-off than you are, do you judge them? Do you judge those who do not seem to be gainfully employed? Remember, we don't know their stories. My perspective is that if I would not want to trade my circumstances with theirs, I should not look down on them, even if it means that I may work harder.*

"I'll pay for it somehow." This story allows you to make purchases without a clear plan for payment, trusting that future income or credit will somehow cover the expense. It's the financial equivalent of magical thinking, and it's how many people find themselves trapped in debt.

- *There is an old expression: We don't plan to fail, but we fail to plan.*
- *Most families (at least three out of every four) live paycheck to paycheck—no matter how much money they earn.*

- *A thousand-dollar emergency might create dire circumstances for you or your family if you don't have an emergency fund. A flat tire, car accident, medical issue, loss of job or reduced work hours are examples.*
- *Student loan debt or credit card debt can be overwhelming.*

"Everyone else has one." This story justifies purchases based on social pressure or the perceived normal standard of living. You convince yourself that you need the latest smartphone, the bigger house, or the expensive vacation because that's what people in your social or economic class are expected to have.

- *Over time, we often think that what were once considered luxuries are actually necessities.*

"I can't change my situation." This story keeps you stuck by convincing you that your financial circumstances are permanent and beyond your control. It might sound like "I'll never make enough money," "I'll always struggle with debt," or "Financial success is for other people, not me."

- *Your circumstance is not your destiny.*
- *Education pays. My education and experience allowed me to earn enough to live on and not have debt. I furthered my education with an MBA in finance, which increased my knowledge and confidence. This allowed me to have a life that was bigger and more interesting than if I had stayed in the small farming town where I graduated from high school. I don't know if I could have earned*

enough to pay for the cost of living if I had not moved and gone to college.

At one point, I was a single mother raising young children. If it were not for my education and work experience in accounting, I might not have been able to provide for them. I got busy, took control of my spending, and was able to create a significant savings account.

The power of these stories lies in their ability to justify behavior that conflicts with your financial well-being. Learning to recognize and challenge these internal narratives is one of the most important skills you can develop on your journey toward financial health. This does not mean everyone needs to have a college degree to find a good job or have a good lifestyle. Having an education was an absolute necessity in the career path that I chose. Statistics show that people with more education earn more money, have more opportunities, and are less likely to be unemployed.

"I don't know what to do." Here are observations that I have had during my life.

- *I know of a young man in his mid-late twenties with a high-paying tech job. In his apartment, he had only a mattress and a television set. He also had a checking account with nine hundred thousand dollars in it. He wasn't earning interest. What was he thinking? Was he thinking about money?*
- *I know a young woman who is a high school graduate, probably nineteen years old, working in a fast-food/beverage retail store, trying to save enough money to get*

reliable transportation and possibly consider furthering her education. She speculates about what she wants to do. She probably doesn't know if her chosen profession will pay her enough to live on, or if there can be job security in this fast-changing world. She doesn't know what to do.

What should she do? What is the first step? What should she do then?

She has a bank account. I suggested that she go to her bank and open a savings account, put in some money, and then ask the bank for a secured credit card with a very small balance. For example, if she had five hundred in the savings account, she could have a credit card with a limit of five hundred dollars. Then, only use the credit card to buy gasoline for her car that she drives to work and food. Make certain to pay it off in full every month on time. After a few months, she would be on her way to establishing a good credit score.

I see the high school girls whose parents work the hardest of anyone in farm fields, but might not know much about helping their children beyond what they know or see in front of them. They may not know about the value of a good education in a stable, well-paying field. Their best advice may be to have their child work putting stickers on fruit that is picked in the fields so that at least they will work in the shade. Once they graduate from high school, they may feel they need to go directly to work to support the family, without furthering their education or finding other opportunities or possibilities. What do I say to these girls? What would I say to their parents, if I could, without sounding like a know-it-all with a superiority complex, if they would even listen to me?

I see people a little older, who have worked hard to have a lifestyle that their parents could have only dreamed of. They live paycheck to paycheck, don't have much saved for retirement, want things they cannot have, want to be generous with their families and others, have a lot of debt, and don't know what to do about it. Their generosity costs them much more than they realize, and it keeps them from being able to be even more generous if they plan their generosity so they do not have debt.

In our next chapter, we'll explore how these stories connect to deeper questions of identity and worth—understanding not just what stories you tell yourself about money, but why you need those particular stories and how they connect to your fundamental sense of self.

Your financial transformation begins with the recognition that you are the author of your money story. You have the power to write a better version, starting today.

CHAPTER 4

The Identity Sources That Mislead Us

> The greatest thing in the world is to know how to belong to oneself.
>
> —Michel de Montaigne

The Identity Crisis Behind Financial Struggles

Who are you? It's one of the most fundamental questions humans ask, yet most of us answer it by describing what we do, what we own, who we know, or how we appear to others. We've learned to define ourselves by external markers that can change, disappear, or prove inadequate at any moment.

This wouldn't just be a philosophical problem if it stayed in the realm of self-reflection. But here's the critical connection: where you derive your sense of identity directly determines how you spend, save, earn, and think about money. When your identity depends on external factors, your financial decisions become desperate attempts to maintain or enhance those identity markers rather than wise choices for your long-term well-being.

See it: Imagine your sense of self as a house. If the foundation is built on shifting sand (external factors like job titles, possessions, or others' opinions), every storm threatens to topple the entire structure. When your identity house shakes, you spend money frantically trying to shore up the walls instead of addressing the unstable foundation.

Feel it: Think of identity like your center of gravity. If your center of gravity is located outside your body—in your job, your stuff, your relationships—you're constantly off-balance, stumbling around trying to regain stability. Financial decisions become desperate grabs for something to steady yourself rather than confident steps toward your goals.

Hear it: Consider identity as the background music of your life. If that music is being controlled by external DJs (bosses, social media, consumer culture), the soundtrack keeps changing unpredictably. One day it's triumphant, the next day it's anxious, and you're constantly spending money trying to get the music back to a song you like.

Why Identity Matters for Money

Your sense of identity affects every financial decision because it determines what feels necessary versus optional, what feels like authentic self-expression versus wasteful spending, and what feels like wise investment versus foolish risk.

Consider two people with identical incomes and expenses, but different identity foundations.

SB derives her identity from being seen as successful and put-together. She spends money on designer clothes, expensive meals out, and a luxury car because these purchases feel essential to maintaining her sense of self. When money gets tight, she feels like she's losing who she is.

DT derives his identity from his values of creativity and authenticity. He spends money on art supplies, experiences that inspire him, and supporting causes he cares about. When money gets tight, he finds free ways to express his creativity and still feels like himself.

Same financial constraints, completely different emotional experiences and spending patterns—all because of how they define themselves.

The Most Common Misleading Identity Sources

Let's examine the four most common external identity sources and how they create financial problems.

Identity Source #1: Work Identity

"I Am What I Do."

What It Looks Like

When meeting new people, you lead with your job title. Your mood depends on how work is going. Your sense of worth fluctuates with professional achievements or setbacks. You introduce yourself by saying "I'm an accountant" or "I work in marketing" rather than sharing your interests, values, or personality traits.

How It Develops

From childhood, we're asked, "What do you want to be when you grow up?" We're not asked, "What kind of person do you want to become?" or "How do you want to contribute to the world?" Our educational system and culture reinforce the idea that career equals identity and that professional achievement determines personal worth.

Real-Life Examples

JW, a software engineer, says, "I spent three thousand dollars on a MacBook Pro and expensive software because real developers use premium tools. I eat lunch out every day with colleagues because networking is essential. I lease a Tesla because, in tech, your car reflects your success level. These aren't just expenses—they're investments in my professional identity."

JW earns eighty-five thousand a year but lives paycheck to paycheck because maintaining his "successful tech worker" identity costs nearly his entire salary. When he considers budgeting, it feels like he's considering becoming a different person.

MA, a nonprofit worker, reports, "I tell myself I can't focus on money because caring about wealth would compromise my values-driven career. I drive an old car and live in a tiny apartment, but I also don't save or invest because building wealth feels inconsistent with my identity as someone who prioritizes service over money."

MA's work identity creates both overspending (on causes and activism-related expenses) and underearning (refusing to negotiate salary or seek higher-paying positions because it might seem "sell out").

BT, who was recently laid off from his marketing job, says, "I don't know who I am anymore. For six years, I was the creative guy at the agency. Now I'm just unemployed. I keep spending money on professional development courses and networking events, but I feel like I'm disappearing without my job title."

The Financial Costs of Work Identity

1. **Professional Maintenance Expenses:** Feeling pressure to spend money on clothing, tools, networking, and lifestyle elements that "match" your professional identity.

2. **Career Transition Trauma:** Experiencing emotions that threaten your identity or self-worth, leading to panic spending or depression-driven financial neglect.

3. **Comparison Pressure:** Measuring your worth against colleagues' apparent success, leading to lifestyle inflation to keep up professionally.
4. **Golden Handcuffs:** Staying in unfulfilling but high-paying jobs because leaving would threaten your professional identity.
5. **Negotiation Avoidance:** Not asking for raises or better opportunities because your identity feels tied to being "grateful" or "not greedy."

Industry-Specific Variations

Tech Workers: Pressure to have cutting-edge gadgets, live in expensive cities, and participate in a startup culture lifestyle.

Creative Professionals: Tension between artistic integrity and financial success, leading to either poverty or selling out narratives.

Healthcare Workers: Identity tied to service can create guilt about focusing on personal finances.

Business Professionals: Pressure to display success through possessions and lifestyle choices.

Teachers: Modest salary expectations that become part of professional identity, limiting financial growth.

Why Work Identity Is Dangerous

Your twenties and thirties are when career identity feels most important, but they are also the most unstable. You're establishing professional credibility while industries change rapidly, making work-based identity both compelling and risky. If you are older, you are either comparing yourself to what you had originally expected, comparing yourself to others, or comparing yourself to what you still want to achieve.

Breaking Free from Work Identity

Here are ways to free yourself from thinking that your work defines you.

1. **Separate doing from being:** You do marketing/teaching/nursing—you aren't a marketer/teacher/nurse.
2. **Develop a multifaceted identity:** Cultivate interests, relationships, and values that exist independently of your job.
3. **Budget beyond professional image:** Make financial decisions based on your actual values and goals, not your professional persona.
4. **Plan for career changes:** Because work-based identity is unstable, build financial flexibility that can survive job transitions.

Identity Source #2: Possessions Identity

Here are thoughts to help you overcome possession identity.

"I Am What I Own."

What It Looks Like

Your possessions feel like extensions of your personality. You believe others judge your character based on what you own. You feel differently about yourself when wearing expensive clothes versus cheap ones. Your living space, car, and belongings are carefully curated to communicate who you are.

The Psychology Behind It

Possessions provide immediate, visible identity markers. Unlike internal qualities like kindness or wisdom, possessions can be quickly acquired and easily displayed. They feel like reliable ways to communicate your identity to others and remind yourself of who you want to be.

Real-Life Examples

AT, a recent college graduate, says, "I know I should save money, but I need professional clothes for job interviews, a good laptop for freelance work, and a decent car that won't embarrass me. These aren't luxuries—they're necessities for the person I'm becoming. My student apartment is tiny, but at least it's decorated with things that reflect my style."

While a portion of what she thinks she needs are accurate, AT spends 70 percent of her income on possessions that feel essential to her adult identity. She doesn't recognize that many items she considers "necessities" are actually attempts to purchase confidence and communicate competence.

TR, a sales representative, explains, "My car is basically my mobile office—it needs to impress clients. My clothes, watch, and phone all communicate that I'm successful, which makes clients trust me. I'm not being materialistic; I'm being strategic about my image."

TR's possession-based identity requires constant upgrades. As soon as his car, clothes, or gadgets begin to feel "outdated," his confidence and professional effectiveness seem to diminish, driving a cycle of continuous spending.

SL, a graphic designer, says, "My apartment is my creative space and my portfolio. Everything here reflects my aesthetic and artistic vision. People can understand who I am just by looking at my space. It's not about showing off—it's about authentic self-expression."

While SL's creative expression through her space brings her joy, she spends more on home décor than on retirement savings and frequently updates her living space when her artistic style evolves, creating a financial drain.

The Hidden Costs of Possessions Identity

1. **Continuous Upgrading:** Your identity requires constant maintenance through new purchases.
2. **Storage and Maintenance:** More possessions require more space, insurance, and upkeep.
3. **Decision Fatigue:** Constantly evaluating possessions' alignment with your desired identity is exhausting.
4. **Attachment Anxiety:** Fear of losing possessions creates stress about theft, damage, or financial changes.
5. **Comparison Escalation:** Others' possessions become threats to your identity rather than neutral objects.

The Social Media Amplification

Platforms like Instagram and TikTok have turned possessions into personal brand elements. Your living space, outfits, and belongings become content that represents you to hundreds or thousands of people, intensifying the pressure to own identity-appropriate items.

Cultural Messages That Reinforce Possessions Identity

- "Your style reflects your personality."
- "Invest in quality pieces that represent who you are."
- "Your home should tell your story."
- "Dress for the job you want, not the job you have."
- "You can tell a lot about someone by what they own."

While these messages contain some truth, they become problematic when possessions become the primary way you express and understand yourself.

Breaking Free from Possessions Identity

Here are ways to determine your authentic identity, not based on your possessions.

1. **Identify authentic expression versus identity anxiety:** Do you buy things because they bring you joy, or because you think you "should" own them?
2. **Practice gratitude for current possessions:** Regularly appreciate what you already own rather than constantly focusing on what you lack.
3. **Experiment with minimalism:** Try living with less and notice whether your sense of self remains intact.

4. **Focus on experiences over objects:** Build identity through what you do and learn rather than what you own.

Identity Source #3: Status Identity

That word *comparison* again. Here are ways to create your own individual identity.

"I Am Where I Rank Compared to Others."

What It Looks Like

Your sense of worth depends on your position relative to others. You constantly measure your progress against peers, family members, or social media connections. You feel good about yourself when you're "ahead" and bad when you're "behind." Your financial decisions are often motivated by appearing successful rather than achieving personal goals.

The Psychological Appeal

Status provides clear, measurable markers for success. Unlike internal qualities that are hard to quantify, status markers like salary, neighborhood, or lifestyle provide concrete ways to assess whether you're "winning" at life. They also promise social benefits like respect, admiration and belonging.

Real-Life Examples

KY, a marketing manager, says, "Most of my college friends are buying houses, so I felt like I had to buy one too. I ended up purchasing something I could barely afford because I couldn't be the only one still renting. Now I'm house-poor, but at least I can say I'm a homeowner. When people ask where I live, I feel proud instead of embarrassed."

KY's status-driven purchase created financial stress but eliminated social anxiety. He prioritized appearing successful over actual financial security, a common pattern when identity depends on relative positioning.

RC, in human resources, explains, "I feel so behind my friends who work in tech and finance. They're making six figures while I'm making forty grand. I can't afford their lifestyle, but I try to keep up when we go out. I put dinners and trips on credit cards because I can't bear to say I can't afford it and look like the poor friend."

RC's status anxiety drives her to spend money she doesn't have to maintain her position in her friend group. She doesn't recognize that her friends might respect her honesty about financial limitations more than her attempts to keep up.

JJ, who is a consultant, says, "I worked so hard to get this job and this salary. I need to look the part—expensive suits, nice apartment in the right neighborhood, new car. These aren't just purchases. They're symbols of my achievement. If I lived cheaply, it would feel like I'm wasting all my hard work."

JJ equates lifestyle inflation with deserved success. He can't separate the satisfaction of achievement from the spending that seems to represent that achievement, leading to lifestyle choices that prevent wealth building despite high income.

The Status Treadmill

Status is relative, which means it's never permanently satisfying. Once you achieve a certain level, you become aware of the next level up. The colleague with a nicer car, the friend with a bigger apartment, the social media connection with better vacations—there's always someone else to measure yourself against.

How Status Identity Creates Financial Problems

This list is about the typical ways that our identity can cause us money problems.

1. **Lifestyle Inflation:** Every income increase automatically leads to spending increases to maintain relative position.
2. **Debt Accumulation:** Using credit to afford status symbols you can't pay for with cash.
3. **Investment Avoidance:** Money that could build long-term wealth gets spent on short-term status displays.
4. **Career Pressure:** Taking high-stress, high-paying jobs primarily for status rather than fit or satisfaction.
5. **Relationship Strain:** Competition with friends and family over lifestyle markers.

The Social Media Status Crisis

Platforms like TikTok, LinkedIn, Instagram, and Facebook provide constant exposure to others' status markers. You see career announcements, vacation photos, home purchases, and lifestyle displays from hundreds of connections, creating an amplified sense of competition and inadequacy.

Special Challenges for Young Adults

Your twenties and thirties are when status differences become most apparent among peer groups. College friends who started at similar points begin earning different salaries, moving to different cities, and achieving different milestones at different paces. This natural divergence can create status anxiety that drives poor financial decisions.

Breaking Free from Status Identity

Determine what values are important to you and compare yourself only to those. Here are ways to overcome status identity issues.

1. **Define success personally:** Create your own metrics for a well-lived life rather than accepting cultural definitions.
2. **Practice gratitude for your path:** Focus on your own growth and progress rather than constant comparison.
3. **Limit social media exposure:** Reduce time on platforms that trigger status anxiety.
4. **Build genuine relationships:** Cultivate friendships based on mutual support rather than competition.
5. **Focus on net worth over appearance:** Measure financial progress by wealth building rather than lifestyle display.

Identity Source #4: Relationship Identity

We are all children, and we may also be siblings, neighbors, co-workers, spouses, or members of organizations. We all seek authentic relationships—and we should. But we are more than those relationships.

"I Am Who Others Think I Am."

What It Looks Like

Your sense of self depends heavily on others' approval and opinions. You make financial decisions based on what will make others happy or impressed. You avoid disappointing family members who have certain expectations. You spend money to maintain relationships or project an image that will win acceptance.

The Psychological Appeal

Humans are social creatures who need belonging and acceptance. Relationship-based identity feels safer than independent identity because it provides external validation and connection. It also seems generous and community-minded rather than selfish.

Real-Life Examples

EB, a recent MBA graduate, says, "My parents sacrificed so much to help me get through school. They expect me to have a successful lifestyle now—nice apartment, professional wardrobe, impressive job. When they visit, I want them to see that their investment paid off. I can't let them know I'm struggling financially because it would break their hearts."

EB spends money she doesn't have to maintain an image of success for her parents. She doesn't realize that her parents would prefer her financial security over their perception of her success.

AL, who is a social worker, states, "My friends expect me to join them for expensive dinners, concerts, and trips. If I don't participate, they'll think I'm cheap or antisocial. I'd rather go into debt than lose these relationships. They're worth more than money to me."

AL doesn't recognize that true friends would understand and accommodate his financial situation. His fear of rejection leads to spending that creates genuine financial problems.

JR, just in a new relationship, says, "I want my girlfriend to know she's important to me, so I take her to expensive restaurants and buy her nice gifts. I can't afford it, but love requires sacrifice. If I acted cheap, she might think I don't care about her or that I can't provide for a future together."

JR confuses financial sacrifice with romantic expression. He doesn't realize that financial stress from overspending could damage the relationship more than modest spending would.

How Relationship Identity Creates Financial Problems

1. **People-Pleasing Spending:** Using money to buy approval, affection, or acceptance.
2. **Gift Guilt:** Feeling obligated to spend more than you can afford on presents for others.

3. **Social Pressure Participation:** Joining group activities that strain your budget to maintain relationships.
4. **Family Expectations:** Meeting relatives' lifestyle expectations rather than your own financial goals.
5. **Conflict Avoidance:** Spending money to avoid difficult conversations about financial limitations.

The Hidden Costs

When your identity depends on others' opinions, you might see the following:

- You can't make authentic financial decisions that align with your values.
- You're vulnerable to manipulation by people who recognize your approval needs.
- You experience anxiety when you can't afford to meet others' expectations.
- You may build resentment toward people you're trying to please.
- You miss opportunities to build genuine relationships based on mutual understanding.

Cultural Variations

Different cultures and families have different expectations around money and relationships.

- Some cultures emphasize family financial support and sacrifice.
- Others prioritize individual financial independence.

- Dating cultures vary in expense expectations.
- Professional networks have different gift-giving and entertainment norms.

Breaking Free from Relationship Identity

1. **Practice authentic communication:** Be honest with trusted people about your financial situation and limitations.
2. **Set boundaries:** Learn to say no to financial requests or expectations that harm your well-being.
3. **Find low-cost ways to show care:** Express love and friendship through time, attention, and thoughtfulness rather than expensive gestures.
4. **Build relationships that accept the real you:** Cultivate connections with people who appreciate you regardless of what you can afford.
5. **Separate love from spending:** Recognize that healthy relationships don't require financial sacrifice.

The Compound Problem: When Identity Sources Overlap

Most people don't rely on just one external identity source—they combine several, creating compound financial problems.

Example: The Triple Threat

AL works in public relations (work identity), drives a luxury car she can't afford (possessions identity), and maintains an expensive lifestyle to impress colleagues and friends (status identity + relationship identity).

AL's spending serves multiple identity needs simultaneously, making it extremely difficult to change any single financial habit. Giving up the car feels like losing professional credibility, personal style, and social status all at once.

Why External Identity Sources Are Ultimately Unsatisfying

All external identity sources share common problems that make them unreliable foundations for self-worth.

Instability: Jobs change, possessions break or become outdated, status is relative and shifting, relationships evolve and sometimes end.

Control: You can't fully control others' opinions, market forces that affect your career, or comparison groups that determine your relative status.

Inadequacy: External sources never provide lasting satisfaction—there's always more achievement, more stuff, higher status, or more approval to seek.

Vulnerability: When external identity sources are threatened or lost, your entire sense of self feels at risk.

Inauthenticity: Living for external validation means you're not living as your true self, creating internal discord and resentment.

Build Internal Identity Foundation

The alternative to external identity sources isn't isolation or selfishness—it's building a sense of self based on internal, stable factors that can weather external changes.

Characteristics of Healthy Internal Identity

What is a healthy internal identity? Here are some ideas.

Values-Based: Your identity centers on what matters most to you—integrity, creativity, service, growth, etc.

Growth-Oriented: You see yourself as someone who can learn and develop rather than someone defined by current circumstances.

Contribution-Focused: Your identity includes how you positively impact others and the world.

Present-Moment Grounded: You find worth in who you are now rather than constantly seeking worth through achievement.

Spiritually Rooted: Whether through religious faith or not, you connect to something larger than material circumstances.

Steps for Identity Transformation

Here are practical steps to modify your identity thinking.

Step 1: Identity Audit

Complete this sentence multiple ways: "I am someone who...."

- Notice how many answers depend on external factors (job, possessions, others' opinions).
- Identify answers that reflect internal qualities (values, character traits, growth mindset).

Step 2: Values Clarification

- List your top five values—the principles that matter most, regardless of circumstances.
- Consider how your financial decisions could better align with these values.

Step 3: Internal Scorecard

Instead of measuring yourself against others, create personal metrics.

- Am I living according to my values?
- Am I growing as a person?
- Am I contributing positively to others?
- Am I making decisions that my future self will appreciate?

Step 4: Financial Alignment

Review your spending patterns.

- Which expenses serve external identity needs versus authentic self-expression?
- Where could you redirect money from impression management to values-based spending?
- How could financial decisions better reflect your internal identity?

Faith-Based Identity

Faith offers a particularly powerful alternative to external identity sources. Scripture teaches that your identity comes from being God's child, created in His image, loved unconditionally and called to specific purposes.

Identity Anchors

- "I am fearfully and wonderfully made" (Psalm 139:14).
- "You are a chosen generation, a royal priesthood, a holy nation" (1 Peter 2:9, NKJV).
- "God will meet all of your needs according to the riches of his glory in Christ Jesus" (Philippians 4:19).

This identity foundation makes financial decisions less anxious for these reasons:

- Your worth doesn't depend on career success or financial achievement.
- You can find contentment regardless of income level.
- Generosity becomes natural because you're secure in God's provision.
- Material possessions become tools for stewardship rather than identity markers.

Create Meaningful Identity

You can build an internal identity foundation through the following:

Personal Philosophy: Develop clear beliefs about what makes life meaningful and how you want to contribute.

Character Development: Focus on becoming the kind of person you respect—honest, kind, brave, etc.

Legacy Thinking: Consider how you want to be remembered and what impact you want to have.

Growth Mindset: See yourself as someone who can learn, adapt and improve throughout life.

Service Orientation: Find ways to contribute to causes larger than yourself.

The Financial Freedom of Internal Identity

When your identity is based on internal rather than external factors, several positive financial changes typically occur.

Reduced Pressure Spending: You don't need to buy things to maintain your sense of self.

Better Decision-Making: Financial choices become clearer when they're based on values rather than image management.

Increased Contentment: You can find satisfaction with "enough" rather than constantly needing more.

Greater Generosity: Security in your identity makes it easier to share resources with others.

Long-Term Focus: You can prioritize wealth building and goal achievement over short-term image concerns.

Relationship Improvement: Authentic relationships develop when you're not constantly trying to impress others.

Career Flexibility: You can make job choices based on fit and values rather than just status and income.

Common Challenges in Identity Transformation

Here are ways to overcome obstacles in your identity improvement.

Fear of Disapproval: Others might not understand or support your shift away from external identity sources.

Old Habit Persistence: It takes time to develop new patterns of thinking about yourself and money.

Social Pressure: Consumer culture and social media constantly reinforce external identity messages.

Identity Confusion: Letting go of external identity sources can temporarily feel disorienting.

Perfectionism: Trying to change identity and financial patterns perfectly rather than gradually.

Move Forward: Your True Identity

The journey from external to internal identity foundation is one of the most important personal development tasks you can undertake. It affects not only your financial life but your career satisfaction, relationship quality, mental health, and overall life fulfillment.

Remember that this isn't about becoming indifferent to others or ignoring practical realities. It's about finding your center of gravity within yourself so that external circumstances can inform your decisions without controlling them.

Your money will always reflect your identity. The question is whether that identity will be based on shifting externals that require constant maintenance and defense, or on internal foundations that provide stability and authentic self-expression.

In our next chapter, we'll explore how the comparison trap—one of the most pervasive identity threats in our digital age—specifically undermines financial well-being and how to break free from its influence.

The person you are at your core, stripped of job titles and possessions and others' opinions, is already valuable, already worthy, already enough. Your financial life becomes much simpler and more satisfying when it flows from this truth rather than constantly trying to prove it through external achievements.

Conclusion Chapter Four

Where do we typically derive our sense of identity and worth? Understanding these sources helps explain why financial struggles often feel like personal failures and why changing our relationship with money requires more than just budgeting techniques.

- **Work Identity** ties our worth to our job title, salary, or professional achievements. When we introduce ourselves, we often start with what we do for work, as if our career defines who we are as people. This creates vulnerability when job situations change or when we compare our career progress to others.

Possessions Identity derives worth from what we own. The car we drive, the house we live in, the clothes we wear, and the gadgets we carry become extensions of our personality and indicators of our success. This identity source is particularly expensive to maintain because it requires constant upgrading and comparison.

Status Identity focuses on our position relative to others. Are we keeping up with our neighbors? Do we appear successful to our colleagues? Can we afford the lifestyle of our peer group? This identity source is exhausting because it's entirely dependent on external validation and comparison.

Relationship Identity ties our worth to who we're connected to or what others think of us. We might overspend to maintain friendships, buy expensive gifts to show love, or live beyond our means to avoid disappointing family members who have certain expectations.

The problem with all these identity sources is that they're external, unstable, and ultimately unsatisfying. Your job can be eliminated, your possessions can be lost or become outdated, your status can change, and relationships can shift. When your identity is tied to these external factors, your financial decisions become desperate attempts to maintain an image rather than wise choices for your long-term well-being.

CHAPTER 5

The Comparison Trap

Comparison is the thief of joy.

—Theodore Roosevelt

In prior chapters, I have written about comparison. This chapter goes even deeper.

Comparison is about pride.

Only compare yourself to yourself. Are you improving?

Imagine walking through life wearing special glasses that automatically highlight everyone else's financial successes while dimming your own achievements. These glasses make other people's possessions look shinier, their careers more impressive, their relationships more fulfilling, and their lives more exciting than yours. You can't take the glasses off because they've been surgically attached to your mind by years of social conditioning and digital exposure.

This is what living in the comparison trap feels like—and it's the single most destructive force affecting your financial well-being in the twenty-first century.

See it: Picture comparison as a funhouse mirror that distorts reality. When you look at yourself, the mirror makes you appear smaller, less successful, and more flawed. When you look at others through this same mirror, they appear larger, more accomplished, and happier. The mirror creates an optical illusion, but your brain processes it as reality.

Feel it: Think of comparison as trying to run a race where the finish line keeps moving. Every time you think you're making progress, you look around and see that others seem to be farther ahead, so you sprint harder, exhaust yourself, and still feel like you're falling behind. The race never ends because it's not really about reaching a destination—it's about the futile attempt to be "ahead" of others.

Hear it: Consider comparison as background noise that drowns out your inner voice. There's a constant chatter telling you what others have, what you lack, how you measure up, and why you should feel inadequate. This noise is so persistent that you can't hear your own thoughts about what actually matters to you or what would genuinely make you happy.

The Psychology of Why We Compare

Comparison isn't a character flaw or a sign of weakness—it's a fundamental human tendency that served evolutionary purposes for thousands of years. Our ancestors needed to assess their position within social groups for survival and reproduction. Knowing who had more resources, higher status, or better protection meant the difference between thriving and dying.

But what once helped humans survive in small tribes now creates misery in the modern world. Your brain still runs ancient comparison software, but instead of comparing yourself to fifty to a hundred and fifty people in your village, you're now comparing yourself to hundreds or thousands of people through social media, news, entertainment, and advertising.

The Neurological Reality

When you see someone else's success or possessions, your brain releases stress hormones as if you were facing a genuine threat. The part of your mind responsible for social comparison doesn't distinguish between "this person has something I want" and "this person has something I need to survive." Your body responds with the same fight-or-flight chemicals either way.

The Dopamine Connection

Comparison also triggers dopamine pathways in your brain—the same neurotransmitters involved in addiction. Getting a "win" in comparison (feeling superior to someone else) provides a chemical reward, while "losing" creates withdrawal-like symptoms. This makes comparison both compulsive and never truly satisfying.

The Digital Amplification Crisis

Social media has turned comparison from an occasional human tendency into a constant psychological assault. Every platform is designed to maximize engagement by triggering emotional responses—and comparison is one of the most powerful emotional triggers available.

The Algorithmic Conspiracy

Social media algorithms are specifically programmed to show you content that creates strong emotional reactions, including envy, inadequacy, and FOMO. The more you engage with comparison-triggering content—even negatively—the more the algorithm serves it to you.

The Curation Illusion

Every social media post is curated content—carefully selected, edited, filtered, and timed for maximum impact. You're comparing your full reality (including struggles, failures, and mundane moments) to others' financial highlight reels. It's like comparing your rough draft to someone else's published novel.

Real-Life Examples of Digital Comparison Damage

SC, scrolling through Instagram, says, "My feed is full of people my age traveling to exotic locations, buying designer clothes, and eating at expensive restaurants. I'm living paycheck to paycheck, but everyone else seems to be thriving. I must be doing something wrong with my life."

SC doesn't realize that many of those travel posts are from people going into debt for Instagram-worthy experiences, the designer clothes might be bought on credit or borrowed, and the expensive restaurant meals might be rare splurges rather than regular lifestyle choices.

JT, checking LinkedIn, laments, "All my college classmates seem to be getting promoted, starting companies, or making six figures. I like my job, but I feel like such a failure seeing everyone else's career announcements. Maybe I should quit and find something more impressive."

JT is comparing his internal experience (knowing his job's challenges and limitations) to others' external presentations (carefully crafted professional updates that highlight only successes).

The False Intimacy Problem

Social media creates the illusion of knowing people intimately while actually providing only surface-level glimpses. You see someone's vacation photos but not their credit card debt. You see their career announcement but not their stress and anxiety. You see their relationship milestones but not their private struggles.

The Financial Cost of Comparison

Comparison doesn't just make you feel bad—it drives specific financial behaviors that can devastate your long-term financial health.

Lifestyle Inflation Through Comparison

Lifestyle inflation is spending more—just because our income increased—not because we need to.

What It Looks Like

Every time you see someone else with something "better" than what you have, you feel pressure to upgrade your own possessions or lifestyle. This creates a constant cycle of spending that escalates regardless of your actual needs or financial capacity.

Real-Life Examples

AG started her marketing career earning forty-five thousand dollars and driving a reliable 2015 Honda Civic. After seeing colleagues with newer, more expensive cars, she traded up to a 2019 BMW, increasing her monthly payment from zero to four hundred and fifty dollars. When she got promoted and saw directors driving luxury SUVs, she traded up again to a sixty-five-thousand-dollar Range Rover with a monthly payment of over eight hundred dollars.

Now earning seventy-five thousand a year, AG spends over ten thousand annually on car payments alone—money that could have built significant wealth if invested instead.

She justifies each upgrade as "keeping up with professional expectations," but the real driver is comparison anxiety.

The Keeping-Up Spending Spiral

Comparison creates artificial urgency around purchases that aren't actually needed. You buy things not because they improve your life, but because not having them makes you feel "behind" relative to others.

Common Comparison-Driven Purchases

- Upgrading phones when yours works fine because others have newer models
- Buying expensive workout clothes because fitness influencers wear designer athletic wear
- Purchasing home décor to match Pinterest-perfect spaces you see online
- Leasing luxury cars to match colleagues' vehicles
- Taking expensive vacations because friends post travel content
- Buying designer clothes to match fashion bloggers' wardrobes

The Hidden Psychology

Each comparison-driven purchase provides temporary relief from inadequacy feelings, but the relief fades quickly because of the following:

1. Someone else always has something "better."

2. Your reference group adjusts upward as your lifestyle improves.
3. The underlying comparison mindset remains unchanged.
4. New comparison triggers constantly emerge through social media exposure.

Debt Accumulation for Image Management

When comparison drives spending beyond your means, credit becomes the bridge between what you can afford and what you feel you "need" to keep up. This creates debt that serves no practical purpose—it exists purely to manage comparison anxiety.

Real-Life Examples

DS works as a film assistant, earning forty-two thousand dollars a year. His college friends work in finance and tech, earning significantly more. To keep up when they go out together, DS uses credit cards to afford expensive restaurants, bars, and entertainment. He's accumulated fifteen thousand in credit card debt purely to maintain his position in his social group.

The monthly minimum payments consume 12 percent of his take-home pay, and the interest charges mean he's essentially paying extra money for the privilege of appearing financially equal to friends who earn twice his salary.

Investment Avoidance Through Comparison Overwhelm

Comparison can also paralyze financial decision-making. When you constantly see others making different investment choices, buying different things, or achieving different milestones, you might avoid making any financial decisions because every option seems inadequate compared to what others are doing.

Example:

RB has twenty thousand dollars in savings but can't decide how to invest it. She sees friends buying real estate, others investing in individual stocks, some starting businesses, and others putting money in retirement accounts. Every option seems wrong because someone else always seems to be doing better with a different strategy. So, she leaves the money in a savings account earning 0.5 percent while inflation erodes its purchasing power.

The Relative Deprivation Phenomenon

One of the cruelest aspects of the comparison trap is that it can make objectively fortunate people feel poor. Researchers call this "relative deprivation"—feeling disadvantaged not because of your actual circumstances, but because of how you perceive yourself relative to others.

The Income Relativity Study

Research shows that people earning fifty thousand dollars in communities where the average income is forty thousand report higher life satisfaction than people earning sixty thousand in communities where the average income is eighty. Your sense of financial well-being depends more on your relative position than your absolute position.

Real-Life Examples

Case Study 1: The Manhattan Lawyer

JN earns a hundred and eighty thousand dollars as a first-year associate at a law firm. In most of America, this would make her wealthy. But in Manhattan, surrounded by partners earning millions, clients with inherited wealth, and a social scene centered around expensive restaurants and activities, she feels financially stressed and inadequate.

Case Study 2: The Silicon Valley Engineer

MG earns a hundred and fifty thousand as a software engineer, more than 85 percent of Americans. But in Silicon Valley, where housing costs are extreme, and colleagues earn over three hundred thousand, he feels like he's struggling financially. He can't afford to buy a home, save significantly, or live the lifestyle he sees around him daily.

The Peer Group Problem

Your sense of financial adequacy depends heavily on your reference group. Change your reference group, and your feelings about your finances change dramatically, even if your actual situation stays identical.

The Social Media Comparison Epidemic

Different social media platforms trigger different types of comparison, each creating specific financial pressures.

Instagram: The Lifestyle Comparison Platform

Do you compare yourself to the Instagram or TikTok version of someone else?

What It Triggers

Visual comparison around lifestyle, possessions, experiences, and appearance. Everything looks perfect, curated, and expensive.

Financial Impact

- Pressure to travel to photogenic destinations
- Spending on clothes, accessories, and beauty products for photos
- Expensive dining experiences that photograph well
- Home décor purchases to create Instagram-worthy spaces
- Fitness and beauty treatments to match filtered appearances

Real User Experience: "I used to be happy with simple weekend activities, but after following travel and lifestyle influencers, staying home feels boring and inadequate. I've started booking expensive weekend trips I can't afford because I want something interesting to post about."

—AM

LinkedIn: The Professional Achievement Platform

Frequently, people have used LinkedIn for career development and job hunting. These can be good uses. However, here are other considerations.

What It Triggers

Career comparison around job titles, salary levels, professional achievements, and business success.

Financial Impact

- Pressure to accept high-stress, high-paying jobs for status
- Expensive professional development courses and conferences
- Designer clothing and accessories for a professional image
- Costly networking events and business lunches
- Pressure to start businesses or side hustles to appear entrepreneurial

Facebook: The Life Milestone Platform

Maybe you used to use Facebook, or even still do. Many people in the world use it regularly.

What It Triggers

Comparison around major life achievements like homeownership, marriage, children, and family success.

Financial Impact

- Pressure to buy homes before financially ready
- Expensive wedding and family milestone celebrations
- Gift-giving pressure for others' milestones
- Lifestyle inflation to match family and friend networks

TikTok: The Instant Gratification Platform

There has been a lot of discussion in the media about the safety of TikTok. United States Presidents have expressed concern about its security. This platform is newer than Facebook and is very widely used. There are potential problems.

What It Triggers

Comparison around youth, trends, viral success, and an immediate-gratification lifestyle—rather than lasting gratification.

Financial Impact

- Constant small purchases of trending items
- Beauty and fashion spending to match viral trends
- Pressure to create content, requiring equipment and setup costs
- FOMO spending on experiences and products featured in viral videos

The Comparison Trap Across Different Life Stages

The comparison trap doesn't only affect us when we are teenagers or young adults. People at all ages and stages of life do it.

The Foundation Formation

Here are thoughts for you when you are just mature enough to think about forming your own identity.

Comparison Triggers

- Different levels of family financial support
- Spring break trips and study abroad opportunities
- Designer clothes and the latest technology
- Internship prestige and career preparation activities

Financial Impact

Student loans increase as students try to maintain lifestyles that match those of their peers with more family support. Credit card debt begins accumulating for social activities and image management.

Real-Life Examples

"My roommate's parents pay for everything—tuition, rent, spending money, even vacations. Meanwhile, I work part-time and have student loans. I started using credit cards to keep up with her lifestyle because I couldn't handle feeling like the poor friend all the time."

—KT

Early Career Establishment Phase

Here are thoughts for those of you who have just started out, and ideas about your money identity and want to get yourself established.

Comparison Triggers

- Salary differences among friend groups
- First apartment and living situation choices
- Professional wardrobe and lifestyle requirements
- Dating expenses and social activities

Financial Impact

This is when comparison-driven debt accumulation often peaks. We try to establish lifestyles that match their peer group without considering income differences.

The Achievement Phase

Here are ideas for you when you have established yourself financially and want to reach a certain level of success, however you define success.

Comparison Triggers

- Homeownership and neighborhood choices
- Wedding expenses and family planning
- Career advancement and salary progression
- Investment and wealth building strategies

Financial Impact

Major financial decisions like home purchases become driven by comparison rather than personal financial readiness. Wedding debt and keeping up with married friends' lifestyle inflation create long-term financial problems.

Cultural and Geographic Variations

I have lived in a variety of settings. This includes military bases, small cities, farms, suburbs, and extremely large cities. I have lived in midwestern states, East Coast states, Southern states, and Western states. I have seen variations in how people think about money, and especially about how they show their money—or do not show it. One example is when I left Iowa to move to the Los Angeles/Orange County area. When in Iowa, the farming-based, small-town-lifestyle people did not overtly "show" their wealth. In the big city, it was the opposite. The cars people drove, designer clothes they wore, and so on, were all very obvious—people did "show" their wealth, whether they had it or not (in debt to their eyeballs). Here are considerations for various living environments.

Urban Versus Rural Comparison Pressures

Urban Areas

Higher cost of living, more visible wealth disparity, and greater lifestyle pressure create intense comparison environments. You're constantly exposed to people with more money and higher status.

Rural Areas

Smaller reference groups, but potentially more intense social pressure within those groups. Everyone knows everyone's business, making financial differences more obvious and personally relevant.

Cultural Differences in Comparison

Individualistic Cultures (like the United States)

Emphasis on personal achievement creates comparison around individual success markers like salary, possessions, and lifestyle.

Collectivistic Cultures

More emphasis on family and community success, but still creates pressure to contribute financially to family expectations and social obligations.

Generational Differences

- **Boomers:** Comparison around homeownership, career stability, and retirement security
- **Gen X:** Comparison around work-life balance and family financial security
- **Millennials:** Comparison around experiences, lifestyle flexibility, and social values
- **Gen Z:** Comparison around authenticity, sustainability, and digital influence

The Relationship Between Comparison and Identity

Comparison becomes most dangerous when it intersects with the identity sources we explored in the previous chapter. When your sense of self depends on external factors, comparison becomes an existential threat rather than just a temporary annoyance.

Work Identity + Comparison: If your worth is tied to career success, seeing others' professional achievements feels like personal failure. This drives poor career decisions based on status rather than fit.

Possessions Identity + Comparison: When your stuff represents who you are, others' possessions become threats to your identity. This drives continuous upgrading and acquisition cycles.

Status Identity + Comparison: Because status is relative by definition, comparison becomes constant and unavoidable. You're always measuring your position against others.

Relationship Identity + Comparison: When your worth depends on others' approval, comparison determines how much approval you need to seek through spending and lifestyle choices.

Break Free from the Comparison Trap

Escaping comparison isn't about becoming unaware of others or uninterested in improvement—it's about changing your relationship with comparative information so it informs rather than controls your decisions.

Step 1: Awareness and Recognition

To overcome the burden of the comparison trap, here are steps to take.

The Comparison Audit

For one week, track every time you notice yourself comparing your life to someone else's, ask yourself these questions.

- What triggered the comparison? (Social media post, conversation, observation).
- What specifically were you comparing? (Possessions, achievements, lifestyle).
- How did the comparison make you feel?
- Did the comparison influence any spending or financial decisions?

Common Comparison Triggers to Watch For

- Scrolling social media feeds
- Attending social gatherings or work events
- Shopping in stores or online
- Reading news or entertainment media
- Conversations with friends and family
- Walking through certain neighborhoods
- Visiting other people's homes

Step 2: Reality Check Your Comparisons

What do you compare yourself with? Here are actions to take.

The Full Story Exercise

When you catch yourself comparing, ask these questions.

- What don't I know about this person's full situation?
- What struggles, costs, or downsides might be hidden?
- How might this person's circumstances differ from mine?
- What advantages might I have that aren't visible?

Real-Life Application

Instead of, "She always wears designer clothes and looks so put-together," try "I see her carefully curated public appearance, but I don't know her budget, debt situation, whether she gets family help, if she shops second-hand designer, or what she sacrifices to afford these clothes."

Step 3: Curate Your Information Diet

Just as you watch what you eat, it is important to be selective as to the information you pay attention to.

Social Media Detox

- Unfollow accounts that consistently trigger comparison and inadequacy.
- Follow accounts that inspire without intimidating.
- Use time limits on social media apps.

- Practice "consuming" versus "comparing" when viewing others' content.

Reference Group Evaluation

Consider whether your regular comparison groups are appropriate and helpful.

- Do these people share your values and life situation?
- Are these comparisons motivating or depressing?
- Would different reference groups be more supportive of your goals?

Step 4: Shift from Comparison to Inspiration

Compare yourself to what you really authentically value.

The Inspiration Reframe

Instead of using others' success to feel inadequate, use it as evidence of what's possible.

- "If they can build wealth on a modest income, maybe I can too."
- "Their career change gives me ideas for my own professional development."
- "Their lifestyle choices show me different options I hadn't considered."

Learning Versus Competing

Approach others' choices with curiosity rather than competition.

- What strategies are they using that I could adapt?

- What can I learn from their approach?
- How might their experience inform my decisions?

Step 5: Develop Internal Measurement Systems

How do you know if you are making progress? It helps to measure it.

Personal Progress Tracking

Instead of measuring yourself against others, measure yourself against your past self.

- Am I making better financial decisions than last year?
- Have I learned new skills or developed better habits?
- Am I closer to my personal goals?
- Do I have more peace about money than before?

Values-Based Evaluation

Regular self-assessment based on your principles rather than external comparisons.

- Am I living according to my values?
- Are my financial choices aligned with what matters most to me?
- Am I making decisions that my future self will appreciate?
- Do I feel good about how I'm using my resources?

Strategies for Comparison-Free Financial Decisions

The goal is to make decisions about money that are not influenced by the negative aspects of comparison. The following methods actually work.

The Blinders Technique

When making major financial decisions, temporarily ignore what others are doing and focus only on your situation.

- What can I actually afford?
- What aligns with my values and goals?
- What choice will serve my long-term well-being?
- What would I choose if no one else would ever know about it?

The Ten-Year Test

Before comparison-driven purchases, ask yourself these questions.

- Will this matter to me in ten years?
- Will I be glad I spent this money when I'm older?
- How will this purchase affect my long-term financial goals?
- What would my future self tell me to do?

The True Cost Calculation

Before buying something to "keep up," calculate the full cost.

- Purchase price + interest (if financed) + maintenance + opportunity cost.
- What else could this money do for me?
- What financial goal will this purchase delay or prevent?
- Is managing comparison anxiety worth this cost?

The Authenticity Check

Ask yourself the following:

- Am I buying this because I genuinely want it, or because others have it?
- Does this purchase reflect my authentic preferences and values?
- Would I want this if I were the only person who would ever see it?
- Am I trying to solve an internal problem with an external purchase?

Special Considerations for Different Groups

Contentment Versus Comparison

Rather than using comparison, I suggest that you seek contentment. This is a process that works over time rather than a one-time fix. I have found that it works, but it has taken time, and sometimes I need to reevaluate and make adjustments. Here are ideas for you, no matter your value system.

Spiritual

- "But godliness with contentment is great gain" (1 Timothy 6:6).
- "Keep your lives free from love of money and be content with what you have" (Hebrews 13:5).
- "Let us not become conceited, provoking and, envying each other" (Galatians 5:26).

Application

- Practice gratitude as a spiritual discipline.
- Remember that your worth comes from God, not possessions or achievements.
- Use prayer to address comparison anxiety.
- Focus on stewardship rather than accumulation.
- Find identity in being God's child rather than in relative status.

Common Faith-Based Comparison Traps

- Comparing ministries or spiritual achievements.
- Church social hierarchies based on giving or service.
- Lifestyle expectations (schooling, family size, etc.).
- Missionary or ministry financial sacrifice comparisons.

Find Meaning Beyond Comparison

Practical identity values include the following:

Approaches

- Develop a personal philosophy about what makes life meaningful.
- Practice mindfulness and present-moment awareness.
- Focus on contribution and impact rather than accumulation.
- Build identity around character development and personal growth.
- Find community with people who share your values.

Meaning-Making Alternatives to Comparison

- Creative expression and artistic development
- Environmental or social cause involvement
- Skill mastery and lifelong learning
- Relationship depth and community building
- Personal challenge and adventure

For Different Income Levels

People who experience life at various income levels have different realities when it comes to comparison to others. Here are a few thoughts.

Lower Income

Comparison can be particularly painful when basic needs are difficult to meet while seeing others' abundance.

Focus on the following:

- Celebrating small progress and improvements
- Finding free or low-cost sources of joy and fulfillment
- Building skills and education for future opportunities
- Connecting with others who share similar circumstances

Middle Income

The most comparison-vulnerable group is the one that has enough to compare but not enough to "win" most comparisons.

Focus on the following:

- Defining success personally rather than culturally
- Appreciating your actual good fortune relative to global standards
- Using comparison as motivation for specific, achievable goals
- Building wealth through boring, consistent strategies rather than flashy ones

Higher Income

Can still experience comparison anxiety with even wealthier groups.

Focus on the following:

- Using resources for meaningful purposes rather than status display

- Understanding the responsibility that comes with financial advantage
- Finding satisfaction in contribution rather than accumulation
- Modeling healthy financial behavior for others

The Relationship Benefits of Comparison-Free Living

When you stop constantly comparing yourself to others, your relationships improve dramatically.

Authentic Connections: You can be genuine about your circumstances rather than managing an image.

Reduced Resentment: You stop feeling bitter toward people who have more than you do.

Increased Generosity: Security in your own situation makes it easier to celebrate others' success.

Better Communication: You can have honest conversations about money and goals.

Deeper Friendships: Relationships based on mutual understanding rather than competition.

Family Harmony: Less tension around lifestyle differences and expectations.

The Creative and Professional Benefits

Being rid of comparison thinking actually frees you to focus your energy on something productive. Here are options:

Career Development: Making job choices based on fit and values rather than status comparisons.

Entrepreneurial Freedom: Starting businesses based on passion and opportunity rather than comparison pressure.

Creative Expression: Pursuing interests and hobbies for personal fulfillment rather than social media content.

Learning Orientation: Focusing on skill development rather than appearing knowledgeable.

Risk-Taking Ability: Making bold choices without worrying about others' opinions.

Long-Term Wealth Building Without Comparison

Run your own race. Don't look at your past or your present. Determine what your authentic values are, and then you can achieve success based on your own definition of success.

Investment Consistency: Making regular investments regardless of what others are doing with their money.

Budget Adherence: Sticking to spending plans based on your goals rather than others' lifestyle choices.

Career Patience: Building skills and experience gradually rather than job-hopping for status.

Lifestyle Stability: Avoiding lifestyle inflation driven by social or family pressure.

Goal Achievement: Staying focused on personal financial objectives rather than competing with others.

Move Forward: Your Comparison-Free Financial Life

Breaking free from the comparison trap is one of the most liberating things you can do for both your finances and your mental health. When you stop measuring your worth against others, you suddenly have permission to make decisions based on what actually works for your life.

The Liberation Process

1. **Recognition:** Becoming aware of when and how you compare yourself to others
2. **Reality Checking:** Understanding the incomplete and curated nature of comparative information
3. **Redirection:** Focusing on personal growth and values-based decisions
4. **Relationship Healing:** Building authentic connections based on mutual support
5. **Financial Freedom:** Making money decisions that serve your actual well-being

What Comparison-Free Financial Life Looks Like

- Contentment with "enough" while still working toward goals
- Financial decisions based on your values and circumstances

- Genuine celebration of others' success without feeling threatened
- Peace about your progress, even when it's different from others'
- Money choices that reflect authentic preferences rather than social pressure

Remember, the goal isn't to become unaware of others or uninterested in learning from them. It's to transform comparison from a source of anxiety and poor decisions into a source of inspiration and information that serves your authentic goals.

Conclusion Chapter Five

Perhaps no force is more destructive to financial peace than comparison. We compare our clothes, cars, homes, vacations, and lifestyle choices to those of others, often to people who are in entirely different financial situations or life stages. Social media has made this problem exponentially worse by giving us a curated window into the financial highlight reels of hundreds or thousands of other people.

The comparison trap is particularly cruel because it's based on incomplete information. You see someone's new car, but not their car payment. You see their vacation photos, but not their credit card debt. You see their beautiful home, but not their stress about the mortgage payment. You're comparing your full financial reality—including your struggles, fears, and limitations—to someone else's carefully selected public image.

This trap leads to what researchers call "relative deprivation"—feeling poor not because of your actual circumstances, but because of how you perceive yourself relative to others. Someone making fifty thousand a year might feel wealthy in one community and poor in another, not because their actual financial situation changed, but because their comparison group changed.

- Comparing ourselves to others.
- Keeping up with the Joneses.
- Needing approval.
- Feeling peer pressure, especially if it is negative, could hurt you or someone else, or would go against your values, wants, and needs.
- Comparing ourselves to the Instagram or TikTok version of someone else.
- Having cultural expectations.
- Getting your identity from work, school, your degree, position, or title.
- Do you work for self-esteem—so you matter?
- Do you get self-esteem from your salary?

The antidote to comparison isn't to ignore others entirely—we naturally learn from observing those around us. Instead, it's to recognize that everyone's financial journey is different, everyone faces challenges that aren't visible from the outside, and everyone has a unique set of resources, responsibilities, and goals that make direct comparison meaningless.

In our next chapter, we'll explore the crucial distinction between needs and wants—a skill that becomes much clearer once you've freed yourself from the comparison trap and can evaluate your true requirements for a fulfilling life.

The most successful and satisfied people aren't those who win the comparison game—they're those who stop playing it altogether and focus on playing the game of their own authentic, values-driven life.

CHAPTER 6

Understanding Needs Versus Wants

> The secret of happiness, you see, is not found in seeking more, but in developing the capacity to enjoy less.
>
> —Socrates

What you require versus what you desire.

The Foundation of All Financial Wisdom

If you could master only one financial skill in your entire life, it should be the ability to distinguish between genuine needs and manufactured wants. This distinction is the foundation of every other financial capability—budgeting, saving, investing, and generous giving all become exponentially easier when you can accurately identify what you actually require versus what you simply desire.

Yet this seemingly simple concept has become one of the most challenging aspects of modern financial life. We live in a culture specifically designed to blur the line between needs and wants, where marketing messages convince us that our desires are actually necessities and where yesterday's luxuries become today's "essentials."

Reality check: For most of human history, 80–90 percent of people lived in extreme poverty. It wasn't until after the Industrial Revolution that many people had more financial resources. In the twentieth century, after the World Wars, the Gilded Age ended. It was replaced by the Production Age, and employees (especially those in trade unions) were able to earn more as productivity increased, resulting in a middle-income class. Children were expected to be financially better off than their parents. Globally, extreme poverty declined dramatically when China and India developed their economies. In recent decades, the rise in productivity of workers has not been matched with increased incomes. With dramatic increases in top executive salaries, it has meant a return to the Gilded Age. It is no wonder that people now wonder what is in store for them and are unsure and anxious about their financial futures. It is important to remember that even now, about 10 percent of people on the planet live in extreme poverty.

See it: Imagine your financial life as a house. Needs are the foundation, walls, and roof—the structural elements you can't live without. Wants are everything else—the decorations, upgrades, and additions that make the house more comfortable or attractive but aren't required for shelter. When you spend your foundation money on decorations, the whole house becomes unstable.

Feel it: Think of needs versus wants like the difference between fuel and accessories in your car. Fuel is what makes the engine run—you can't get anywhere without it. Accessories like premium sound systems, leather seats, or custom wheels might enhance the experience, but they're not required for transportation. When you spend your fuel money on accessories, you're stranded regardless of how nice your car looks.

Hear it: Consider needs versus wants as the difference between the melody and the harmony in a song. The melody carries the essential tune—you need it to have a song at all. Harmony adds richness and beauty, but it's built on top of the melody. When you focus so much on harmony that you lose the melody, the music becomes chaotic and unsatisfying.

The Hierarchy of Human Needs

To understand what you truly need, it's helpful to understand how human needs work psychologically. Psychologist Abraham Maslow's hierarchy of needs provides a useful framework, though I'll adapt it for modern financial reality.

Level 1: Physiological Needs (Survival Requirements)

These are the absolute basics required for human survival.

- **Air and water:** Generally free in developed countries, but quality matters
- **Food:** Nutrition for basic health and energy
- **Shelter:** Protection from elements and safety from harm
- **Sleep:** A safe, quiet place to rest
- **Basic healthcare:** Emergency medical care and preventive health maintenance
- **Financial Reality:** For most people, these needs can be met at various price points, but they cannot be eliminated entirely without serious consequences.

Level 2: Safety and Security Needs

Once survival needs are met, humans need the following:

- **Physical safety:** Personal security and protection from violence
- **Financial security:** Enough resources to maintain basic needs consistently
- **Health security:** Access to healthcare and health insurance
- **Employment security:** Reliable income source
- **Emergency preparedness:** Resources for unexpected challenges

Financial Reality: Security needs require planning and saving beyond immediate survival, but they don't require luxury-level spending.

Level 3: Love and Belonging Needs

Humans are social creatures who need the following:

- **Relationships:** Family, friendship, and romantic connections
- **Community:** Sense of belonging to groups that share values or interests
- **Social acceptance:** Feeling valued and included by others
- **Communication:** Ability to connect and share with others
- **Financial Reality:** These needs can often be met with minimal financial cost, though consumer culture tries to convince us otherwise.

Level 4: Esteem Needs

People need to feel the following:

- **Self-respect:** Confidence in their abilities and worth
- **Achievement recognition:** Acknowledgment of accomplishments
- **Independence:** Ability to make their own choices
- **Status:** Respected position within social groups
- **Financial Reality:** This is where needs and wants begin to blur, because esteem can be built through

expensive status symbols or through free personal development.

Level 5: Self-Actualization Needs

At the highest level, humans need the following:

- **Purpose:** Sense of meaning and direction in life
- **Creativity:** The ability to express themselves and create
- **Growth:** Continuous learning and development
- **Contribution:** Ways to make a positive impact on others
- **Financial Reality:** Self-actualization often requires minimal money but maximum intentionality and personal development.

The Consumer Culture Manipulation

Understanding human needs wouldn't be so complicated if we lived in a vacuum, but we're surrounded by a $600 billion advertising industry specifically designed to make wants feel like needs. Every marketing message you encounter is crafted to trigger psychological needs while offering product solutions.

How Marketing Creates Artificial Needs

Safety Manipulation

- Insurance ads that create fear about unlikely disasters

- Security system marketing that amplifies crime anxiety
- Investment advertisements that play on retirement fears
- Health and beauty products that create body insecurity

Belonging Manipulation

- "Everyone who matters" uses this product
- Brand communities that promise social acceptance
- Status symbols that claim to communicate your values
- Social media advertising that targets your friend groups

Esteem Manipulation

- "You deserve this" messaging that ties products to self-worth
- "Professional" versions of basic items that suggest competence
- Luxury marketing that promises increased confidence
- Achievement rewards that require an expensive celebration
- VIP status options for everything you buy or do

Self-Actualization Manipulation

- Products that promise to help you "find yourself"
- Experiences marketed as essential for personal growth
- Tools and services that claim to unlock your potential
- Lifestyle brands that offer identity rather than just products

Real-Life Examples of Need Manipulation

The Professional Wardrobe Trap

LS just started her first hotel management job, earning forty-five thousand dollars a year. She receives messages that she needs a "professional wardrobe" to be taken seriously. Marketing tells her she needs designer suits, expensive handbags, and quality shoes to succeed professionally.

Reality: LS needs clean, appropriate clothing for her workplace. This can be achieved with a few versatile pieces from affordable retailers, totaling between five and eight hundred dollars, rather than the three to five thousand suggested by fashion marketing.

The Fitness Identity Crisis

MS decides to get in shape. Fitness marketing convinces him he needs a premium gym membership (at eighty dollars a month), designer workout clothes (another three hundred), protein supplements (a hundred per month), a fitness tracker (four hundred dollars), and a meal delivery service (two hundred per month) to achieve his health goals.

Reality: MS needs movement and proper nutrition. This can be achieved with bodyweight exercises, running, basic clothing, and home-cooked meals at a fraction of the marketed cost.

The Social Connection Confusion

RJ feels lonely in a new city. Social marketing suggests she needs to join expensive fitness classes, eat at trendy restaurants, attend costly events, and buy fashionable clothes to make friends and build community.

Reality: RJ needs genuine human connection, which can often be found through free community groups, volunteering, hobby clubs, religious organizations, and outdoor activities that cost little or nothing.

Distinguish Between Genuine Needs and Manufactured Wants

Learning to separate authentic needs from consumer-created wants requires developing what we might call "need discernment"—the ability to see through marketing messages and social pressure to identify what you actually require for well-being.

The Need Authentication Process

Before any significant purchase, ask yourself these questions:

1. **The Survival Test**
    - Will my health, safety, or basic functioning be compromised without this?

- Am I trying to meet a physiological need or a psychological want?
- Can I survive and thrive without this item for another month/year?

2. **The Alternative Test**

- Are there free or low-cost ways to meet this same need?
- Have I explored all alternatives before choosing the expensive option?
- Am I buying convenience, status, or actual necessity?

3. **The Time Test**

- Have I wanted this for more than thirty days, or is this a sudden desire?
- Will I still want this in six months, or is this a temporary impulse?
- Am I responding to immediate pressure or long-term planning?

4. **The Values Test**

- Does this purchase align with my stated values and priorities?
- Am I spending money on what matters most to me, or on what others expect?
- Would my future self be grateful for this purchase?

5. **The Full Cost Test**

- Can I afford the purchase price, maintenance, storage, and eventual replacement?
- What opportunity cost am I accepting by spending money on this?
- Am I considering only the immediate cost or the total lifetime expense?

Common Want-to-Need Transformations

Consumer culture is skilled at making wants appear to be needs. Here are common examples.

Transportation

- **Need:** Reliable way to get to work, essential appointments, and basic activities.
- **Want:** New car, luxury vehicle, status symbol car, multiple vehicles.
- **Marketing Message:** "You need reliable transportation" (true), "so you need a new car" (false).
- **Reality:** Reliable transportation can be achieved with used cars, public transit, biking, or car-sharing, depending on your situation.

Communication

- **Need:** Ability to communicate with family, friends, and work.
- **Want:** Latest smartphone, premium data plans, multiple devices.

- **Marketing Message:** "Stay connected" (important) "with our premium service" (unnecessary).
- **Reality:** Communication needs can be met with basic phone plans and older devices that function perfectly well.

Food

- **Need:** Adequate nutrition for health and energy.
- **Want:** Gourmet ingredients, dining out frequently, convenience foods, and social eating experiences.
- **Marketing Message:** "You deserve good food" (true), which means expensive food" (false).
- **Reality:** Nutritional needs can be met deliciously and adequately with home cooking and basic ingredients.

Housing

- **Need:** Safe, clean shelter with basic amenities.
- **Want:** Luxury finishes, prestigious location, maximum space, designer furnishings.
- **Marketing Message:** "Your home reflects who you are" (partially true), "so it needs to be impressive" (false).
- **Reality:** Housing needs can be met in various ways that don't require premium costs.

Education and Growth

- **Need:** Skills and knowledge for personal and professional development.

- **Want:** Expensive courses, premium programs, status-brand education.
- **Marketing Message:** "Investment in yourself" (good concept) "requires expensive training" (often false).
- **Reality:** Learning needs can often be met through free or low-cost resources, libraries, online courses, and self-directed study.

The Lifestyle Inflation Problem

One of the most insidious ways "wants" become "needs" is through lifestyle inflation—the tendency for your expenses to increase whenever your income increases. What once felt like luxuries gradually become necessities in your mind, making it impossible to feel financially secure, regardless of how much you earn.

How Lifestyle Inflation Works Psychologically

It is common to change how we change what we think that we need. In most places today, we think that air conditioning is a need. In some places, it absolutely is. However, a century ago, humans lived without it. Throughout history, items that had originally been considered "luxuries" came to be considered "necessities." As your income increases, it is quite common to decide that what you may now be able to afford is now a need rather than a want.

The Adaptation Effect

Humans adapt quickly to improved circumstances. The luxury apartment that felt amazing in month one becomes your new baseline by month six. You don't feel grateful for the upgrade anymore—you just feel normal, and anything less would now feel like deprivation.

The Reference Group Shift

As your income increases, you tend to associate with people who earn similar amounts. Your new peer group's lifestyle becomes your new comparison standard, making previously adequate choices feel insufficient.

The Identity Integration

Lifestyle improvements become part of your identity. You're no longer someone who "splurged" on premium coffee—you're someone who "drinks good coffee." The behavior transforms from an occasional treat to a personality trait.

Real-Life Lifestyle Inflation Examples

Here is what it looks like.

The Young Professional Progression

Year 1 (Salary: $45,000): "I'm so grateful to afford my own studio apartment and cook most meals at home. Going out to eat feels like a special treat."

Year 3 (Salary: $60,000): "I deserve a one-bedroom apartment in a better neighborhood. I'm too busy to cook much, so meal delivery services make sense for my lifestyle."

Year 5 (Salary: $80,000): "I need a car to advance professionally. My apartment should have a gym and nice amenities because I work so hard. I eat out most days because I don't have time to shop and cook."

Year 7 (Salary: $100,000): "I'm still living paycheck to paycheck somehow. I guess I just need to earn more money to feel financially secure."

Each lifestyle upgrade felt reasonable and justified in the moment, but the cumulative effect consumed every salary increase, leaving her feeling no more financially secure at a hundred thousand than at forty-five thousand.

The Couple Lifestyle Inflation

Dating (Combined income: $90,000): Happy with casual dining, used cars, and simple entertainment.

Engaged (Combined income: $110,000): "We need to look successful for our wedding. Plus, we're combining finances, so we can afford nicer things."

Married (Combined income: $130,000): "We deserve a nice honeymoon after all the wedding stress. And we should live in a place that reflects our marriage, not just our dating life."

Established (Combined income: $160,000): "We're both advancing professionally, so we need reliable cars, a nice home, and a lifestyle that matches our status. Maybe we should start thinking about upgrading everything."

The couple's expenses increased faster than their income, creating financial stress despite earning significantly more than when they were happily living on much less.

The Real Costs of Confusing Needs and Wants

When you consistently treat wants as needs, several expensive problems emerge.

Financial Problems

The primary reason people don't have financial freedom is that what they think they need has a lot of "wants." Here are the reasons it is a problem.

Debt Accumulation: Using credit to afford "necessities" that are actually wants.

Savings Inability: No money left for emergency funds or long-term goals because "needs" consume everything.

Investment Avoidance: Can't build wealth because current "needs" require all available resources.

Income Pressure: Feeling forced to work longer hours or take higher-stress jobs to afford lifestyle "needs."

Retirement Inadequacy: No retirement savings because present "needs" take priority.

Psychological Problems

I am not a trained counselor or therapist, but it is very easy to see the issues that come from the confusion of wants versus needs.

Chronic Dissatisfaction: Never feeling like you have "enough" because wants are unlimited.

Anxiety and Stress: Worry about maintaining lifestyle "needs" creates constant pressure.

Identity Confusion: Tying self-worth to possessions and lifestyle choices rather than character.

Decision Fatigue: Constantly evaluating and reevaluating lifestyle choices exhausts mental energy.

Guilt and Shame: Overspending on wants while calling them needs creates internal conflict.

Relationship Problems

One of the main reasons that marriages fail is money. Here are examples.

Partner Conflicts: Disagreeing about what constitutes genuine needs versus lifestyle wants.

Family Stress: Children learning unhealthy patterns about needs, wants, and money.

Friend Pressure: Feeling obligated to match others' lifestyle choices to maintain relationships.

Generational Tension: Parents or grandparents not understanding your "necessary" expenses.

Social Isolation: Unable to participate in free or low-cost activities because lifestyle "needs" consume resources.

Develop Contentment with "Enough"

The antidote to chronic want-expansion is developing contentment—the ability to find satisfaction with meeting your genuine needs plus some reasonable wants, without constantly craving more.

What Contentment Looks Like Financially

How could it feel to be content with enough?

Needs Coverage: Confident that your basic requirements for health, safety, and well-being are met.

Want Selectivity: Choosing some wants based on values and priorities rather than trying to afford everything you desire.

Future Security: Saving and investing for long-term goals while enjoying present resources reasonably.

Generous Capacity: Having resources available to help others and contribute to causes you care about.

Peace of Mind: Not constantly worried about money or pressured to earn/spend more.

Contentment Strategies

How to get there—having a content mindset.

The Gratitude Practice: Daily acknowledgment of resources, opportunities, and blessings you currently have, rather than focusing on what you lack.

Example: Instead of "I wish I could afford a nicer car," try "I'm grateful my current car gets me where I need to go safely and reliably."

The Abundance Perspective: Recognizing that your lifestyle, even if modest by cultural standards, represents abundance by historical and global standards.

Reality Check: If you have clean water, reliable electricity, internet access, and freedom to make career and lifestyle choices, you have resources that billions of people lack and that no one in human history had access to until recently.

The Values Filter: Making spending decisions based on your personal values rather than cultural expectations or social pressure.

Example: If you value creativity and learning, spending money on art supplies or courses aligns with contentment. If you don't value fashion, expensive clothes won't create lasting satisfaction.

The Experience Priority: Research consistently shows that experiences create more lasting happiness than possessions. Prioritizing experiences over accumulation often leads to greater contentment.

Application: Instead of upgrading your living space, consider spending similar money on travel, classes, or shared activities with people you care about.

Strategies for Need-Versus-Want Decisions

Here are practical steps to make better decisions.

The Thirty-Day Want List

Instead of buying items immediately when you want them, try the following:

1. Write down the item and why you want it.
2. Wait thirty days before purchasing.
3. After thirty days, evaluate whether you still want it and why.
4. If you still want it, determine whether it's a need or a want.
5. If it's a want, decide whether it aligns with your values and budget.

Many items on thirty-day want lists lose their appeal once the initial impulse fades.

The Cost-Per-Use Analysis

For any significant purchase, try the following:

1. Estimate how often you'll use the item.
2. Calculate the cost per use over its lifetime.
3. Consider whether the cost per use justifies the expense.
4. Compare to alternatives with better cost-per-use ratios.

Example: A three-hundred-dollar coffee machine used daily for five years costs about sixteen cents per use. A two-thousand-dollar exercise bike used twice per week for two years costs about $9.60 per use. The coffee machine might be a better value even though it's more expensive initially.

Let's think about the ongoing monthly cost of subscriptions, especially electronic ones. They can be for streaming movies, sporting events, or television shows. Computer gaming can also be quite expensive. Having internet access is a need, but how much and at what speed? How many upgrades do you need to reach the top VIP levels? I suggest that you add these costs and evaluate what you really need and what really gives you joy—perhaps cut down.

The Minimalist Challenge

Periodically practice living with less to rediscover what you actually need.

- Spend a month buying only absolute necessities.
- Try living out of one suitcase for a week.
- Avoid shopping (except for food and essentials) for thirty days.
- Use only basic versions of products you normally upgrade.
- Don't pay more for VIP status.

These exercises help recalibrate your sense of what's truly necessary versus what's simply comfortable.

The Alternative Exploration

Before buying anything, explore alternatives.

- Can you borrow, rent, or share this item instead of buying?
- Is there a free or low-cost way to meet the same need?
- Can you buy a used version for significantly less?
- Would a different approach eliminate the need entirely?

Example: Instead of buying expensive exercise equipment, consider free workout videos, outdoor running, bodyweight exercises, or community sports leagues.

Special Considerations for Different Life Stages

Our financial needs are different throughout our lives. We don't need the same things in our thirties as when we were teenagers. When we are retired, our needs are different from when we are in our twenties. Here are thoughts about differences based on life states.

College Years: Establishing Adult Needs

Here are thoughts for those of you in college, trade school, or learning as you start your work life.

Common Confusions

- Thinking you need the same lifestyle your parents provide

- Treating social activities as necessities for belonging
- Believing you need premium versions of basic items
- Confusing career preparation with lifestyle requirements

Healthy Approaches

- Accept that your needs as a student are different from your parents' needs as established adults.
- Find low-cost ways to build relationships and have fun.
- Buy basic, functional versions of items until you can afford upgrades.
- Invest in education and skills rather than lifestyle symbols.

Early Career: Building Independence

Congratulations, you have completed a lot of learning and are now focused on earning. Here are thoughts for when you are starting out.

Common Confusions

- Thinking you need to look phenomenally successful before you are successful
- Believing professional advancement requires lifestyle inflation
- Treating career-building expenses as unlimited necessities

- Confusing adult independence with expensive independence

Healthy Approaches

- Build professional credibility through competence rather than appearance.
- Invest in skills and relationships rather than status symbols.
- Live below your means while your income grows.
- Define adult success personally rather than culturally.

Established Career: Avoiding Lifestyle Inflation

Now that you have been working and have life experience, there are both more opportunities and obstacles. Here are ideas about wants versus needs at this point.

Common Confusions

- Believing salary increases should automatically become lifestyle increases
- Thinking you "deserve" expensive things because you work hard
- Assuming higher-income people need higher-expense lifestyles
- Treating past luxuries as current necessities

Healthy Approaches

- Increase savings and investments rather than just expenses when income grows.

- Maintain perspective on what constitutes genuine necessity.
- Use extra income for generosity, security, and experiences rather than just accumulation.
- Regularly reassess whether your lifestyle reflects your values or just your income.

Cultural and Religious Perspectives on Needs Versus Wants

The way we think about wants and needs is based not only on our life stage but on our life priorities. Here are ideas based on various perspectives.

Stewardship and Contentment

The Bible has a lot to say about both stewardship and contentment. Here are some verses.

Spiritual Principles

- "Keep your lives free from love of money and be content with what you have" (Hebrews 13:5).
- "But if we have food and clothing, we will be content with that" (1 Timothy 6:8).
- "Better a little with the fear of the Lord than great wealth with turmoil" (Proverbs 15:16).

Applications

- View money as a tool for stewardship rather than personal satisfaction.

- Practice contentment as a spiritual discipline.
- Distinguish between needs (which God promises to provide) and wants (which may or may not align with God's plan).
- Use resources generously while living modestly.
- Find identity in relationship with God rather than possessions or lifestyle.

Challenges

- Avoiding "poverty gospel" that makes financial struggle seem more spiritual
- Balancing wise provision with trust in God's provision
- Distinguishing between legitimate needs and ascetic extremes
- Using freedom to make wise rather than legalistic financial choices
- Avoiding the false "prosperity gospel" that focuses on financial rewards

Values-Based Living

Here are other ideas for money identity based on values.

Philosophical Frameworks

- Minimalism: Finding satisfaction through intentional reduction of possessions
- Stoicism: Focusing on what you can control while accepting what you cannot

- Existentialism: Creating meaning through choices rather than acquisitions
- Environmentalism: Considering sustainability and impact in consumption decisions

Applications

- Define personal values and align spending with those values.
- Focus on experiences, relationships, and personal growth rather than accumulation.
- Consider the environmental and social impact of consumption choices.
- Build identity through character development rather than possession acquisition.
- Find community with others who share similar approaches to consumption.

The Economics of Needs Versus Wants

Wants are much more expensive than needs. That is why they call them wants. Misunderstanding the differences can be very costly—even wasteful.

Personal Economic Impact

It costs you personally.

When You Confuse Needs and Wants

- Higher necessary expenses leave less money for savings and investments.

- Debt accumulation from funding lifestyle "requirements."
- Income pressure to maintain lifestyle standards.
- Financial stress from overcommitting resources.

When You Clearly Distinguish Needs and Wants

- Lower baseline expenses create more financial flexibility.
- Ability to weather income changes or unexpected expenses.
- Resources available for investments and long-term goals.
- Financial peace from living below your means.
- Generosity can be increased as you refocus your priorities.

Societal Economic Impact

It costs us all.

Consumer Economy Dependence

Our economy depends on people spending most of their income on consumption. Clear need/want distinction could theoretically reduce economic activity if adopted widely. Consumer spending is over two-thirds of the economy.

Individual Versus Societal Interests

What's good for your personal financial health (spending less, saving more) might conflict with what's good for economic growth (spending more, saving less). However, increased generosity can improve financial freedom for others.

Finding Balance

You can support economic activity while maintaining personal financial health by doing the following:

- First being generous with money that you earn or receive
- Spending thoughtfully on things you value rather than reducing all spending
- Investing savings in companies and funds that support economic growth, people, and the environment
- Supporting local businesses and conscious consumption based on sustainability
- Choosing quality over quantity in purchases

Advanced Need-Versus-Want Concepts

There are times when it is not exactly clear what the difference is between a want and a need. For example, you need to live in a safe area, but it doesn't have to be the most expensive area in order to be safe. You need proper nutrition, but how much do you need to spend to have appropriate healthy nutrition? Here are situations when there is more complexity.

The Investment Versus Expense Distinction

Certain purchases that seem like wants might actually be needs when viewed as investments.

Education and Skills

- Want: Expensive courses for personal interest.
- Need: Training that significantly improves earning potential.
- Analysis: Calculate potential return on investment. For example,, if two to four years of quality education in a promising field could increase your earning potential by hundreds or thousands of dollars over your work life of forty-plus years, it will be worth the cost of the education, so long as you don't take on too much student debt.

Health and Wellness

- Want: Premium gym membership for social reasons.
- Need: Exercise access for physical and mental health.
- Analysis: Consider long-term healthcare cost prevention.

Professional Development

- Want: Networking events for social enjoyment.
- Need: Industry connections for career advancement.
- Analysis: Evaluate actual professional benefit.

The Quality Versus Price Balance

Sometimes paying more initially saves money long-term.

Durability Considerations

There are times when a product can be functional longer without the need to be replaced, costing less overall.

- Cheap shoes that wear out quickly versus quality shoes that last years
- Reliable used car versus unreliable cheap car.
- Energy-efficient appliances versus cheap appliances with high operating costs

Value Calculations

- Total cost of ownership over the item's lifetime
- Maintenance and replacement costs
- Opportunity costs of time spent dealing with inferior products

The Seasonal and Situational Needs

Your needs aren't static—they change based on circumstances.

Life Stage Changes

- Student needs differ from career needs.
- Single-person needs differ from family needs.
- Healthy people's needs differ from those of people with medical conditions.

Geographic Considerations

- Urban versus rural transportation needs
- Climate-specific clothing and housing needs
- Local cost-of-living variations

Career Requirements

- Some professions genuinely require specific tools or appearance standards.
- There are home office needs for remote workers.
- There are travel requirements for certain jobs.

Build Your Personal Needs Versus Wants Framework

Make this work for you. Here are practical steps that you can take.

Step 1: Baseline Needs Assessment

Create a comprehensive list of your genuine baseline needs.

- Monthly food budget for adequate nutrition
- Housing costs for a safe, clean shelter
- Transportation for essential activities
- Healthcare and insurance costs
- Basic clothing for weather and workplace requirements

Step 2: Values-Based Wants Hierarchy

List wants in order of importance to your values and goals.

- High priority: Wants that align closely with your values
- Medium priority: Wants that provide some value but aren't essential
- Low priority: Wants that don't significantly contribute to your well-being

Step 3: Financial Capacity Reality Check

Determine how much money you can allocate to wants after covering the following:

- All genuine needs
- Emergency fund building
- Long-term savings goals
- Debt payment (if applicable)

Step 4: Regular Review and Adjustment

Every three months, assess the following:

- Have my actual needs changed?
- Are my want priorities still aligned with my values?
- Is my spending reflecting my stated priorities?
- What adjustments would better serve my long-term well-being?

The Freedom of Clear Boundaries

When you can clearly distinguish between needs and wants, several types of freedom emerge.

Financial Freedom: More money available for emergencies, generosity, savings, and investments.

Decision Freedom: Easier choices because you're not constantly debating what's "necessary."

Social Freedom: Less pressure to keep up with others' lifestyle choices.

Career Freedom: Ability to make job choices based on fit rather than just income requirements.

Psychological Freedom: Less anxiety about money and more contentment with your situation.

Time Freedom: Less time spent shopping, maintaining possessions and working to afford lifestyle inflation.

Conclusion Chapter Six

One of the most practical aspects of developing a healthy money identity is learning to distinguish between genuine needs and manufactured wants. This distinction, while simple in concept, can be revolutionary in practice.

Needs are the essentials required for life. Not all of them require money. They include love (sense of belonging), physical (shelter, food, clothing), safety and security, self-esteem and self-respect, fun, play, laughter, information, wisdom, understanding, beauty and aesthetics, fulfillment, self-actualization, freedom, and liberty.

It takes money for shelter, food, clothing, transportation, healthcare, and safety. These represent your non-negotiable expenses—the minimum required for a healthy, dignified life.

"I make myself rich by making my wants few."

—Henry David Thoreau

"May your home always be too small to hold all your friends"

—Old Irish Blessing

Wants are everything else. They're the additions, upgrades, and preferences that make life more comfortable, convenient, or enjoyable, but aren't necessary for survival or basic well-being.

The more money people have, the more items they think they need.

The challenge is that our consumer culture has become incredibly sophisticated at making wants feel like needs. Advertising messages convince us that we "need" the latest technology, that we "deserve" VIP status and premium brands, and that certain lifestyle choices are "necessary" for happiness or success.

This is compounded by lifestyle inflation—the tendency to increase our spending as our income grows, turning yesterday's luxuries into today's necessities. The smartphone that was once a want becomes a need. The car that was once "good enough" becomes inadequate. The home that once felt spacious becomes cramped.

Learning to pause and ask, "Is this actually necessary for my well-being, or is this a want that I've convinced myself is a need?" can transform your financial decision-making. It doesn't mean never spending money on wants—it means making conscious choices about when those expenditures align with your values and financial goals.

Move Forward: Your Needs Versus Wants Mastery

Mastering the distinction between needs and wants is a lifelong practice, not a one-time decision. Consumer culture, changing life circumstances, and social pressures will constantly challenge your clarity about what you truly require versus what you simply desire.

The goal isn't to eliminate all wants from your life—it's to make conscious, values-based decisions about which wants to pursue and which to let go. When your needs are clearly met, and your wants are thoughtfully chosen, money becomes a tool for creating the life you actually want rather than a source of constant pressure and anxiety.

In our next chapter, we'll explore the emotional dimension of money—how feelings drive financial decisions and how to develop emotional intelligence around money that supports your long-term well-being.

Remember: You have everything you need right now to begin living a financially healthy life. Everything else is a choice about how to use your resources wisely and generously in service of your values and goals.

The most financially successful people aren't those who can afford everything they want—they're those who want the right things and can find contentment with enough.

CHAPTER 7

The Emotional Dimension

Money is never just about money. Navigating the complex landscape of early career decisions, relationship formation, and identity development, this truth becomes especially profound. At twenty-two, your emotional relationship with money might center around independence and proving yourself. At twenty-eight, it might focus on security and comparison with peers. At thirty-four, it could involve family responsibilities and long-term planning anxiety. At forty, you may reflect over your life and compare it with what you expected years earlier. At fifty-plus, you may wonder what life will be like after retirement.

Understanding the emotional dimension of your financial life isn't just helpful—it's essential. This is why financial advice that ignores emotions often fails, why budgets based purely on logic frequently get abandoned, and why even financially successful people can feel constantly stressed about money.

The Changed Emotional Landscape for Young People

Young people today face emotional money challenges that previous generations simply didn't encounter on the same scale. You're the first generation to grow up with social media constantly displaying others' financial highlight reels. There is unprecedented student loan debt, housing costs that have outpaced income growth, and a gig economy that offers flexibility but little security.

At the same time, you have access to more financial information, investment options, and entrepreneurial opportunities than any generation before you. This creates a different emotional cocktail: endless possibilities mixed with overwhelming choice; financial opportunity paired with economic uncertainty, and unprecedented access to wealth building tools combined with unprecedented visibility into others' financial success.

The Quarter-Life Financial Crisis

Many young adults experience what psychologists call "quarter-life crisis"—a period of anxiety and uncertainty about career, relationships, and life direction that often occurs in the mid-twenties. This crisis has a significant financial component that previous generations didn't face as intensely.

Consider TM, who graduated with a marketing degree and forty thousand dollars in student loans. She's working at a nonprofit she loves but earns thirty-five thousand annually. Her college roommate just bought a condo and posts Instagram stories from expensive restaurants. TM feels simultaneously proud of her meaningful work and anxious about her financial progress. She loves her job but worries she's "behind" financially compared to her peers.

This internal conflict—between personal values and financial pressure, between authentic choices and societal expectations—creates emotional stress that purely logical financial advice can't address. TM doesn't just need a budget; she needs to understand why money triggers anxiety and how to make financial decisions that honor both her values and her need for security.

How Different Emotions Drive Financial Behavior

Your emotional state significantly influences your financial decisions, often in ways you don't consciously recognize. Understanding these patterns is crucial for developing financial habits that serve your long-term well-being.

Fear-Based Financial Decisions

Fear manifests differently depending on your background and current situation.

Fear of Not Having Enough

This fear might cause you to do the following:

- Work excessive hours at jobs you dislike because you're afraid of financial instability
- Avoid investing because you're terrified of losing money
- Live extremely frugally, even when you can afford enjoyment
- Hoard money in low-yield savings accounts because other options feel too risky

Fear of Missing Out (FOMO)

This fear might drive you to engage in the following behaviors:

- Spend money on experiences you can't afford because everyone else is doing them
- Invest in trendy assets (like cryptocurrency or meme stocks) without understanding their risks
- Upgrade your lifestyle beyond your means to keep up with your peers
- Take on debt for travel, dining, or entertainment to avoid feeling left out

Fear of Judgment

This fear might lead you to do the following:

- Hide your financial struggles from friends and family
- Spend money you don't have to maintain appearances

- Avoid seeking financial help because you're embarrassed about your situation
- Make career decisions based on how they look to others rather than what serves your well-being

Consider WD, who grew up in a family that frequently worried about money. Even though he now has a stable job with good benefits, he experiences anxiety whenever he spends money on anything beyond basic necessities. He has fifteen thousand dollars in a savings account but won't invest any of it because he's terrified of losing money. His fear, while understandable given his background, is actually harming his long-term financial security because inflation is eroding his purchasing power.

Shame and Financial Self-Worth

Shame is perhaps the most destructive emotion in financial life because it drives secrecy, prevents learning, and creates cycles of poor decision-making. Financial shame can stem from lots of places.

Comparison with Peers: Social media creates constant opportunities to compare your financial reality with others' curated success stories. You see friends' new apartments, exotic vacations, and career achievements without seeing their debt, family financial support, or behind-the-scenes struggles.

Family Financial Dynamics: If you grew up in a family where money was scarce, you might feel shame about wanting financial success or enjoying money when you have it. Conversely, if you grew up with financial privilege, you might feel shame about your advantages or pressure to live up to family financial expectations.

Educational and Career Pressure: With rising education costs and competitive job markets, many people feel shame about their career progress, student loan debt, or inability to achieve the financial milestones they expected to reach by certain ages.

Past Financial Mistakes: Credit card debt from college, poor investment decisions, or other financial missteps can create lasting shame that prevents you from taking positive financial action in the future.

AK accumulated twelve thousand dollars in credit card debt during her first job out of college. She was making twenty-eight thousand annually and tried to maintain the lifestyle she'd had as a student with family financial support. The debt created such shame that she avoided looking at her credit card statements for months, which only made the problem worse. Even after paying off the debt three years later, she still feels anxious about any credit card use and has difficulty making financial decisions confidently.

Anger and Financial Resentment

Many people experience anger about financial circumstances, often justified by real systemic challenges.

Economic Frustration: Housing costs, student loan debt, healthcare expenses, and wage stagnation create legitimate anger about economic conditions that previous generations didn't face to the same degree.

Inequality Awareness: Social media and news coverage make wealth inequality more visible than ever, creating anger about unfair advantages and systemic barriers.

Family Financial Dynamics: Resentment toward family members who had different financial opportunities or who made financial decisions that affected your options.

Career and Income Frustration: Anger about job markets, credential inflation, or income levels that don't match educational investment.

While this anger is often justified, it can lead to destructive financial behaviors if not processed healthily.

- Impulsive spending as a form of rebellion
- Avoiding financial planning because the system is rigged anyway
- Making poor investment decisions based on anger rather than analysis
- Sabotaging your own financial progress as a way of rejecting societal expectations

Anxiety and Financial Overwhelm

Financial anxiety among people has reached unprecedented levels. This anxiety often stems from the following:

Information Overload: Access to endless financial advice, investment options, and success stories can create paralysis rather than empowerment.

Uncertainty About the Future: Questions about career stability, economic conditions, climate change, and social security create anxiety about long-term planning.

Immediate Financial Pressure: Student loans, rent, healthcare costs, and other expenses create constant financial stress.

Social and Family Pressure: Expectations about financial milestones, career success, and lifestyle choices create anxiety about measuring up.

This anxiety often manifests in two extremes: either complete avoidance of financial planning or obsessive monitoring of every financial detail. Neither extreme serves your long-term well-being.

The Identity Crisis: Who Am I Without My Money Story?

Money often becomes deeply intertwined with identity development. This creates unique emotional challenges because you're simultaneously figuring out who you are and how money fits into that identity.

Work Identity and Financial Self-Worth

In a culture that often asks "What do you do?" as an opening question, your career becomes central to your identity. This creates emotional challenges in a multitude of situations.

Your Job Doesn't Pay Well: If you're passionate about teaching, social work, nonprofit work, or other meaningful but lower-paying careers, you might feel constant tension between your values and your financial security.

You're Underemployed: Many college graduates work in jobs that don't require their education level or don't utilize their skills, creating frustration and uncertainty about their financial trajectory.

You're in the Gig Economy: Freelancing, contract work and entrepreneurship offer flexibility but create income uncertainty that can be emotionally exhausting.

Your Career Doesn't Match Your Education: Whether due to changing interests, economic conditions, or limited opportunities, many people work in fields unrelated to their education, creating questions about their investment in college and their professional identity.

Consider FM, who has a master's degree in environmental science but works as a barista while looking for relevant employment. He loves environmental work but needs income to pay his student loans and rent. His part-time environmental consulting brings in money, but it's not enough to live on. He feels constantly torn between financial necessity and professional passion, leading to anxiety about both his career and his money.

Lifestyle Identity and Spending Patterns

People often use spending to express identity and values, but this can create emotional and financial conflicts.

Values-Based Spending: You might prioritize organic food, sustainable products, or ethical brands even when they're more expensive, creating tension between your values and your budget.

Experience-Focused Identity: If your identity centers around travel, dining, entertainment, or other experiences, you might struggle with the financial limitations these priorities create.

Minimalist Versus Comfort Tensions: Some people embrace minimalism but find themselves wanting comfort and convenience items, creating internal conflict about their identity and spending.

Social Identity Through Spending: Using purchases to signal group membership, whether through fashion, technology, dining choices, or entertainment preferences.

Emotional Triggers and Spending Patterns

Understanding your personal emotional triggers for spending is crucial for developing financial self-awareness. Common triggers include the following:

Stress Spending

I've done it too. After difficult workdays, relationship conflicts, or major life changes, many people turn to spending for comfort.

- "Retail therapy" to get a quick pick-me-up that doesn't last
- Online shopping late at night when feeling overwhelmed
- Expensive meals or drinks after stressful situations
- Impulse purchases during major life transitions
- Subscription services that provide comfort or entertainment

Celebration Spending

Good news often triggers spending that exceeds the actual cause for celebration.

- Expensive dinners after job promotions that don't justify the cost
- Shopping sprees after achieving goals
- Vacation bookings after receiving bonuses
- Lifestyle inflation after pay increases

Social Spending

Peer pressure and social situations create spending that might not align with your actual preferences or budget.

- Expensive group dinners that strain your budget

- Vacation participation to maintain friendships
- Fashion purchases to fit in with social groups
- Entertainment expenses that exceed your comfort level

Comparison Spending

Seeing others' success or lifestyle choices triggers spending to keep up.

- Home décor purchases after seeing friends' apartments
- Wardrobe updates after seeing professional connections
- Technology upgrades after seeing peers' devices
- Experience purchases after seeing social media posts

The Faith Factor: Different Approaches to Money Emotions

How you approach money emotionally often depends on your broader worldview and belief system.

Spiritual

If faith is important to you, it can provide both comfort and additional complexity around money emotions.

- **Trust Versus Anxiety:** Scripture repeatedly encourages trust in God's provision, but this can create guilt when you feel financial anxiety.

- **Contentment Versus Ambition:** Teachings about contentment might conflict with cultural messages about financial success.
- **Generosity Versus Security:** Desires to be generous might conflict with needs for financial security.
- **Stewardship Versus Enjoyment:** Questions about how much money you should save versus spend or give away.

Emotional Processing

- Prayer as a tool for processing financial anxiety and decisions
- Community support through church relationships
- Wisdom for understanding money's proper role in life
- An eternal perspective that can reduce financial stress

However, faith communities sometimes create additional emotional pressure around money.

- Guilt about financial struggles or prosperity
- Pressure to tithe even when financially struggling
- Judgment about spending choices or career decisions
- Unrealistic expectations about faith solving financial problems

Consider RF, who grew up in a family that emphasized tithing and generous giving. She wants to honor these values but struggles with student loan payments and an entry-level salary. She feels guilty when she can't give as much as she wants to and anxious about her financial security. Her faith provides comfort but also creates additional emotional complexity around money decisions.

Values-Driven Purpose

If you don't identify as religious, you're creating your own moral and emotional framework around money.

- Identifying personal values that guide financial decisions
- Creating meaning and purpose
- Developing personal principles about generosity, success, and security.
- Finding community support

Approaches to Financial Emotions

- Therapy or counseling for processing money-related anxiety or trauma
- Mindfulness and meditation practices for emotional regulation
- Philosophy and literature for wisdom about money's role in a meaningful life
- Scientific approaches to understanding behavioral economics and psychology

Emotional Challenges

- Creating personal meaning around financial choices without guidance

- Finding community support for financial struggles and goals
- Developing principles about generosity and social responsibility
- Processing economic inequality and systemic issues without a framework

Consider TN, who grew up in a family that identifies as agnostic. He's successful in his tech career but feels empty about his work and uncertain about how much money he needs to be happy. Without a religious framework for understanding money's purpose, he struggles to find meaning in his financial success and questions whether his career path aligns with his desire to contribute positively to society.

Process Financial Trauma and Family Money Messages

Many emotional reactions to money stem from family experiences and messages received during childhood and adolescence. Understanding these patterns is crucial for developing healthy adult relationships with money.

Common Family Money Messages

You may have heard or said these things before. They are not all helpful, but they may impact us and others.

Scarcity Messages

- "Money doesn't grow on trees."
- "We can't afford that."

- "Rich people are greedy or corrupt."
- "You have to work hard for every penny."

Success Messages

- "Money equals success."
- "You need to make more than your parents did."
- "Education guarantees financial security."
- "Appearance matters for career advancement."
- "You can't trust anyone with money."

Guilt/Shame Messages

- "Money is the root of all evil."
- "You're being selfish, wanting nice things."
- "Other people have it worse."
- "You should be grateful for what you have."

Security Messages

I actually agree with all of these particular messages for most people.

- "Save for a rainy day."
- "Don't put all your eggs in one basket."
- "Always have an emergency fund."

These messages, whether positive or negative, create emotional reactions that influence adult financial behavior. Understanding your family's money messages helps you choose which to keep and which to replace with healthier perspectives.

Financial Trauma Responses

Some people experienced financial trauma during childhood.

- Parents losing jobs or businesses during formative years
- Families losing homes due to financial difficulties
- Constant fighting about money in the household
- Parents using money as control or punishment
- Experiencing poverty or financial insecurity

These experiences can create lasting emotional responses.

- Hypervigilance about financial security, leading to excessive saving or anxiety about spending
- Avoidance of financial planning because it triggers traumatic memories
- Control issues around money, stemming from childhood powerlessness
- Relationship difficulties when money becomes a trigger for past trauma

Professional counseling can be invaluable for processing financial trauma and developing healthier emotional relationships with money.

Develop Emotional Intelligence Around Money

Emotional intelligence—the ability to recognize, understand, and manage emotions—is crucial for financial well-being. This skill can be developed through intentional practice.

Emotional Awareness Practices

Fortunately, there are things that you can do to have positive emotions about money.

Daily Emotional Check-ins

Before making financial decisions, pause and ask yourself the following:

- What am I feeling right now?
- Is this emotion influencing my financial thinking?
- What would I decide if I were feeling calm and centered?
- Am I making this decision based on logic or emotion?

Spending Emotion Tracking

Keep a brief record of your emotional state when making purchases.

- What was your mood before spending?
- What emotions did the purchase satisfy?
- How did you feel immediately after spending?
- How do you feel about the purchase a day/week later?

Financial Decision Journaling

Write about significant financial decisions, including the following:

- What factors influenced your choice?
- What emotions came up during the decision-making process?
- What fears or hopes were involved?
- How does this decision align with your values and goals?

Emotional Regulation Techniques

Pause Practices

Develop habits that create space between emotional triggers and financial decisions.

- Twenty-four-hour waiting periods for non-essential purchases over a certain amount
- Three deep breaths before checking investment accounts or bank balances
- Walking or other physical activity when feeling financial stress
- Talking with trusted friends before making major financial decisions

Reframing Techniques

Learn to challenge emotional reactions with different perspectives.

- Instead of "I can't afford this," try "I'm choosing to spend my money differently."
- Instead of "I'm behind financially," try "I'm on my own unique path."
- Instead of "I should have more by now," try "I'm making progress toward my goals."
- Instead of "Money is stressful," try "I'm learning to manage money wisely."

Mindfulness Practices

Develop present-moment awareness around money.

- Mindful spending, where you pay attention to purchase decisions
- Gratitude practices that focus on what you already have
- Body awareness to notice physical tension around financial stress
- Breathing exercises when feeling financial anxiety

Build Healthy Emotional Habits Around Money

Developing long-term emotional health around money requires consistent practices and habits.

Regular Financial Emotional Processing

The only way to make any changes is to modify both your beliefs/thinking and your behaviors/habits. Here are options.

Weekly Money Meetings with Yourself

Set aside time each week for the following:

- Review your spending and emotional reactions to it
- Assess progress toward financial goals
- Process any financial stress or anxiety from the week
- Plan for financially challenging situations for the coming week

Monthly Values Check-ins

Evaluate whether your financial choices align with your stated values.

- Are you spending money on things that matter to you?
- Are your financial goals consistent with your life priorities?
- Do your money habits support or undermine your well-being?
- What adjustments might better align your finances with your values?

Quarterly Financial Therapy

Consider deeper emotional work around money.

- Professional counseling for financial anxiety or trauma
- Support groups for financial struggles or goals
- Workshops or courses on financial psychology
- Books or resources about the emotional aspects of money

Community and Relationship Support

As with most things in life, it can be easier and more effective to get help. These techniques might help you.

Financial Accountability Partners

Find trusted friends or family members who can provide the following:

- Emotional support during financial challenges
- Accountability for financial goals and spending habits
- Perspective when emotions cloud financial judgment
- Celebration of financial successes and progress

Professional Support Network

Build relationships with professionals who understand financial emotion.

- Financial planners who consider emotional factors
- Therapists who specialize in financial issues

- Career counselors who understand money and work relationships
- Mentors who model healthy financial and emotional patterns

Creating Emotional Safety Around Money

We all want to feel emotionally safe. In fact, I believe that we all need to feel emotionally safe. Here are ways.

Emergency Emotional Fund

Just as you might have an emergency financial fund, create emotional resources for financial stress:

- List of people to call when feeling financial anxiety
- Practices that calm you during money stress
- Reminders of past financial challenges you've overcome
- Affirmations or principles that ground you during uncertainty

Financial Self-Compassion

Develop kind, understanding approaches to financial mistakes and challenges.

- Treat financial errors as learning opportunities rather than character flaws.
- Recognize that everyone makes financial mistakes.
- Focus on progress rather than perfection.
- Celebrate small financial victories and improvements.

The Path Forward: Integration and Growth

Understanding the emotional dimension of your financial life is not a one-time achievement but an ongoing process of growth and development. As you change and grow, your emotional relationship with money will evolve as well.

Embrace Financial Emotional Maturity

Financial emotional maturity involves the following:

- Self-awareness about your emotional triggers and patterns around money
- Emotional regulation skills that allow you to make decisions based on wisdom rather than impulse
- Value alignment where your financial choices support your deepest priorities
- Relationship health where money enhances rather than damages your connections with others
- Resilience in the face of financial setbacks and challenges
- Generosity that flows from abundance thinking rather than obligation

This maturity develops gradually through experience, reflection, and intentional growth. It's not about eliminating all emotional responses to money—emotions provide valuable information about what matters to you. Instead, it's about learning to work with your emotions rather than being controlled by them.

Your Unique Emotional Money Journey

Remember that your emotional relationship with money is unique to your background, personality, values, and circumstances. What works for others might not work for you, and what worked for previous generations might not fit your situation.

Whether you find strength through faith or not, the goal is to develop financial and emotional patterns that serve your well-being and allow you to use money as a tool for creating the life you actually want.

Your journey toward financial emotional health is not just about improving your relationship with money—it's about developing the self-awareness, emotional regulation, and value clarity that serve every area of your life. The skills you develop around financial emotions will enhance your career decisions, relationships, and personal growth.

The emotional dimension of money is not a problem to be solved but an ongoing aspect of life to be understood and managed wisely. As you continue growing and changing, your emotional relationship with money can become a source of strength, clarity, and positive impact rather than stress and confusion.

Conclusion Chapter Seven

Money is never just about money—it's about the kind of person you're becoming and the kind of life you're creating. Understanding its emotional dimension is essential for both financial success and personal fulfillment. It's about security, freedom, self-worth, relationships, and dreams. This is why financial problems feel so personal and why financial advice that ignores the emotional dimension often fails.

Consider how different emotions drive different financial behaviors.

Fear might cause you to hoard money, avoid investing, or make overly conservative financial choices that actually harm your long-term security.

Shame about past financial mistakes or current circumstances might prevent you from seeking help, learning new skills, or making necessary changes.

Anger about unfair circumstances, income inequality, or past financial betrayals might lead to impulsive spending or risky financial decisions.

Anxiety about an uncertain future might drive you to either save compulsively or spend impulsively, depending on how you cope with stress.

Guilt about having more or less than others, about past spending, or about financial priorities might cloud your judgment and prevent you from making clear-headed decisions.

Understanding your emotional relationship with money helps explain why logical financial advice doesn't always translate into changed behavior. You might know intellectually that you should save more and spend less, but if your emotions are driving your financial decisions, knowledge alone won't be enough to create change.

CHAPTER 8

Self-Worth and Money

Don't confuse your work with your worth. Your value as a human being is not dependent upon what you own. This simple statement contains one of the most revolutionary truths you can embrace: your inherent worth exists completely separate from your financial circumstances, career achievements, or material possessions.

This separation feels nearly impossible to maintain. You've grown up in a culture where net worth and self-worth have become dangerously intertwined, where your Instagram feed doubles as a financial report card, and where "What do you do?" and "How much do you make?" feel like assessments of your value as a person.

Breaking this link isn't just about feeling better—it's about financial freedom. When your self-worth depends on your financial status, every financial decision becomes an identity crisis. You make choices based on what will make you look successful rather than what serves your actual well-being. You take on debt to maintain an image, avoid opportunities because you're afraid of financial judgment and measure your progress against impossible standards set by social media's financial highlight reels.

The Modern Identity Crisis: When Money Becomes Who You Are

You face a new set of challenges in separating identity from financial status. Previous generations often stayed in the same jobs, communities and social circles for decades. Your identity markers were more stable and less performance-based. Today, you're expected to constantly reinvent yourself, build your personal brand and prove your worth through visible achievements.

The Performance Economy

You're living in what researchers call the "performance economy," where your value is constantly being measured, rated, and displayed.

- Your LinkedIn profile becomes a performance of professional success.
- Your social media feeds curate your lifestyle achievements.
- Your resume must tell a story of constant upward mobility.

- Your spending choices signal your values, taste, and status.
- Your living situation reflects your career progress and life choices.

This constant performance pressure creates what psychologists call “contingent self-worth,” where your value as a person feels dependent on external achievements and acquisitions. When your self-worth is contingent on financial success, you become trapped in cycles of anxiety, comparison, and never feeling “enough.”

Consider GR, a graphic designer earning forty-five thousand dollars annually. She loves her creative work but feels embarrassed about her salary when friends discuss their jobs. She’s accumulated eight thousand in credit card debt trying to maintain a lifestyle that looks successful on social media. She avoids dating because she’s ashamed of her small apartment and old car. Her financial choices aren’t serving her actual needs—they’re serving her perceived need to appear successful to others.

The Comparison Trap Amplified

Social media has created unprecedented opportunities for financial comparison. You see friends’ vacation photos without seeing their credit card debt, colleagues’ promotions without seeing their work-life balance struggles, and influencers’ luxury purchases without seeing their authentic income sources.

This comparison culture creates several destructive patterns.

Lifestyle Inflation Beyond Means: Feeling pressure to match others' visible spending even when your income doesn't support it.

Career Anxiety: Constant comparison with peers' career progress, creating anxiety about your own path.

Achievement Pressure: Feeling like you should have reached certain financial milestones by specific ages.

Authenticity Loss: Making choices based on how they'll appear to others rather than what genuinely serves you.

Imposter Syndrome: Feeling like a fraud when your financial reality doesn't match your external presentation.

The Cost of Tying Worth to Wealth

When your self-worth becomes dependent on your financial status, the consequences extend far beyond your bank account.

Emotional and Mental Health Impacts

Chronic Anxiety: When your value as a person feels tied to financial performance, every financial decision becomes loaded with emotional weight. Checking your bank account becomes an assessment of your worth as a person.

Depression and Shame: Financial setbacks don't just affect your circumstances—they feel like personal failures that reflect your inadequacy as a human being.

Perfectionism: The need to maintain a perfect financial image prevents you from taking healthy risks, learning from mistakes, or seeking help when needed.

Isolation: Shame about financial circumstances leads to social withdrawal and an inability to form authentic relationships.

Decision Paralysis: When every choice carries identity weight, decision-making becomes overwhelming and exhausting.

Relationship Consequences

Authentic Connection Difficulties: When you're performing financial success, you can't form genuine relationships because others don't know the real you.

Dating and Romance Stress: Financial insecurity creates anxiety about whether you are "worthy" of love, leading to either avoiding relationships or entering them with unhealthy dynamics.

Friendship Strain: Inability to be honest about financial limitations damages friendships and creates stress around social activities.

Family Tension: Pressure to meet family expectations about financial success creates conflict and distance from loved ones.

Career and Financial Decision Impacts

Risk Avoidance: When your identity depends on financial security, you avoid healthy risks that could lead to growth and opportunity.

Values Misalignment: Making career choices based on salary and status rather than fulfillment and contribution.

Debt Accumulation: Using credit to maintain an image rather than making sustainable financial choices.

Delayed Financial Goals: Spending money on appearance instead of building actual wealth.

Entrepreneurship Fear: Avoiding business opportunities because failure would feel like personal inadequacy.

Understand True Worth Versus Net Worth

Breaking the link between self-worth and money requires understanding what actually determines your value as a human being.

Inherent vs. Contingent Worth

There is a difference between inherent worth that everyone automatically has and contingent worth that depends upon something like what you do or what you have.

Inherent worth is your value as a human being simply because you exist.

This worth is all of the following:

- Unchanging regardless of circumstances
- Not dependent on achievements or failures

- Present from birth until death
- Unaffected by external validation or criticism
- The foundation of healthy self-esteem

Contingent worth is a value that depends on external factors.

This includes the following:

- Career success and salary levels
- Educational achievements and credentials
- Social status and peer approval
- Material possessions and lifestyle markers
- Performance in various life areas

Healthy individuals recognize that they are inherently worthwhile, working toward goals and achievements without making their value contingent on outcomes.

Faith Foundations

If faith is important to you, Scripture provides clear foundations for understanding your worth apart from worldly achievements.

Created in God's Image: "So God created mankind in his own image, in the image of God he created them" (Genesis 1:27). Your worth comes from bearing God's image, not from your bank account balance.

Loved Unconditionally: "God demonstrates his own love for us in this: While we were still sinners Christ died for us" (Romans 5:8). God's love for you isn't based on your success or failure—it's based on His character.

Chosen and Valued: "You are a chosen generation, a royal priesthood, a holy nation" (1 Peter 2:9, NKJV). Your identity comes from being chosen by God, not from your career or possessions.

Provided For: "God will meet all your needs according to the riches of his glory in Christ Jesus" (Philippians 4:19). Your security comes from God's provision. Your ability to accumulate wealth comes from God.

Consider LM, a youth pastor earning thirty-two thousand dollars annually. He struggled with shame about his salary when college friends discussed their corporate jobs. Through studying biblical principles about identity and worth, he learned to find security in his calling and God's love rather than in salary comparison. This shift allowed him to make financial decisions based on wisdom rather than insecurity.

Other Foundations

You can develop strong foundations for inherent worth.

Human Dignity: Philosophical traditions across cultures recognize inherent human dignity that doesn't depend on achievements or possessions.

Personal Values: Your worth can be grounded in your commitment to values like kindness, integrity, creativity, justice, and contribution to others.

Relationships and Love: Your capacity to love and be loved by family, friends, and romantic partners reflects your inherent worth as a person.

Growth and Learning: Your ability to learn, grow, and develop throughout life demonstrates your inherent value independent of current circumstances.

Contribution and Service: Your potential to contribute positively to the world gives you worth regardless of your current financial status.

Consider BN, who works as a social worker earning thirty-eight thousand dollars per year. She initially felt embarrassed about her modest salary compared to friends in tech and finance. Through therapy and personal reflection, she learned to ground her worth in her values of service and her meaningful relationships rather than salary comparisons.

Steps to Separate Worth from Wealth

Breaking the link between self-worth and money requires intentional practices and mindset shifts.

Daily Practices for Worth Recognition

Changing your mind can change your behavior. The opposite is also true. Changing your behavior/habits can also change how you think.

Morning Affirmations: Begin each day by acknowledging your inherent worth.

- "My value as a person is not determined by my bank account."
- "I am worthy of love and respect regardless of my financial circumstances."
- "My worth comes from who I am, not what I own."
- "I make financial decisions based on wisdom, not insecurity."

Gratitude Beyond Money: Practice gratitude that focuses on nonfinancial blessings.

- Relationships that bring you joy
- Personal qualities you appreciate about yourself
- Experiences that have shaped you positively
- Ways you've grown and learned
- Contributions you've made to others

Values Clarification: Regularly remind yourself what actually matters to you.

- What qualities do you most admire in people you respect?
- What achievements make you feel genuinely proud?
- What experiences bring you the most satisfaction?
- How do you want to be remembered by others?
- What legacy do you want to leave beyond financial success?

Reframe Financial Conversations

Change how you think and talk about money to separate it from identity.

Instead of: "I can't afford that" (implies personal inadequacy).
Try: "I'm choosing to spend my money differently" (emphasizes choice and values).

Instead of: "I'm broke" (identity statement).
Try: "I'm currently managing a tight budget" (temporary circumstance).

Instead of: "I'm not successful" (identity judgment).
Try: "I'm working toward my financial goals" (process focus).

Instead of: "I should be making more by now" (self-judgment).
Try: "I'm on my own unique path" (acceptance of individual journey).

Build Financial Confidence Independent of Net Worth

Feeling financially free is having confidence that you will be ok. It is not all about how much you have.

Competence Over Comparison

Focus on developing financial skills rather than comparing your situation to others.

- Learn about budgeting, investing, and money management.

- Celebrate improvements in your financial knowledge.
- Take pride in making wise decisions regardless of the amounts involved.
- Measure progress against your past self, not against others.

💡 ***Many jackpot winners, elite athletes, and celebrities lose all their money as they are not prepared to make good financial decisions when they receive huge amounts of money.***

Values-Based Decision-Making

Make choices based on your priorities rather than external expectations.

- Spend money on things that align with your values.
- Save for goals that matter to you personally.
- Choose careers based on fulfillment of your values as well as financial considerations.
- Give generously in ways that reflect your priorities.

Process Over Outcomes

Focus on your efforts and choices rather than just results.

- Celebrate consistent budgeting even when money is tight.
- Take pride in learning from financial mistakes.
- Appreciate the discipline of saving even small amounts.

- Value wise spending decisions regardless of your total wealth.

Address Common Worth-Wealth Confusion Areas

Certain life situations commonly trigger worth-wealth confusion.

Career and Salary Anxiety

Young people face a new set of career pressures that can tie identity to professional success.

The Passion Economy Pressure: You're told to "follow your passion" while also needing to earn a living wage, creating identity conflicts when passion doesn't pay well.

Credential Inflation: Many jobs now require degrees that weren't necessary for previous generations, creating anxiety about educational investment and career returns.

Gig Economy Uncertainty: Freelancing and contract work offer flexibility but create income unpredictability that can trigger identity insecurity.

Comparison Culture: Constant visibility into peers' career progress through LinkedIn and social media amplifies comparison anxiety.

Strategies for Career-Worth Separation

- Define success broadly to include fulfillment, work-life balance, and contribution, not just salary.
- Remember that a career is what you do, not who you are.
- Celebrate skill development and learning regardless of current position.
- Find meaning in your work beyond just financial compensation.
- Build identity around your values and character, not your job title.

Social Media and Lifestyle Presentation

Social platforms create constant pressure to present a financially successful image.

The Financial Highlight Reel Problem: Everyone presents their best moments, creating unrealistic comparison standards.

Lifestyle Inflation Pressure: Seeing others' purchases and experiences creates pressure to match their spending.

Financial Performance Anxiety: Fear that your authentic lifestyle isn't impressive enough to share.

Strategies for Social Media Health

- Curate your feeds to include authentic, diverse perspectives.

- Share honestly about your real life, including financial challenges.
- Take regular breaks from social media when it triggers comparison.
- Remember that online presentations rarely reflect the complete reality.
- Focus on real-life relationships over online validation.

Dating and Relationships

Financial insecurity can severely impact romantic relationships.

Dating Anxiety: Worry that you're not financially stable enough to date or that potential partners will judge your circumstances.

Relationship Inequality: When partners have different income levels or life experiences, it creates insecurity and identity conflicts.

Future Planning Stress: Anxiety about whether you're financially prepared for relationship milestones like marriage or homebuying.

Strategies for Relationship Health

- Be honest about your financial circumstances with potential partners.
- Look for partners who value your character over your wealth.

- Communicate openly about financial goals and values.
- Remember that healthy relationships involve mutual support through various circumstances.
- Focus on building a strong partnership rather than competing financially.

Family and Peer Pressure

Family expectations can create significant worth-wealth confusion.

Generational Pressure: Parents or grandparents who expect you to achieve certain financial milestones by specific ages.

Sibling Comparison: Family dynamics that compare siblings' financial success.

Cultural Expectations: Communities that measure success primarily through financial achievement.

Peer Group Pressure: Friends whose lifestyles or career choices create implicit pressure to match their spending or achievement levels.

Strategies for Managing External Pressure

- Have honest conversations with family about your values and goals.
- Set boundaries around financial discussions that feel judgmental.

- Choose friends who accept you for who you are, not what you earn.
- Remember that you don't need to justify your choices to others.
- Focus on living according to your values rather than others' expectations.

Build a Healthy Money Identity

Creating a positive relationship with money while maintaining healthy self-worth requires developing what psychologists call "financial self-efficacy"—confidence in your ability to manage money wisely regardless of your current wealth level.

Components of Financial Self-Efficacy

Knowledge Confidence: Believing you can learn what you need to know about money management, investing, and financial planning.

Decision Confidence: Trusting your ability to make financial choices that align with your values and goals.

Recovery Confidence: Knowing that you can bounce back from financial mistakes and setbacks.

Growth Confidence: Believing that your financial situation can improve through wise choices and persistent effort.

Relationship Confidence: Feeling capable of healthy financial communication in relationships and families.

Develop Financial Self-Efficacy

Believing that you have the ability to be successful is a powerful mindset.

Start Small

Build confidence through small financial wins.

- Successfully managing a simple budget for a month
- Saving even small amounts consistently
- Making wise spending decisions on everyday purchases
- Learning one new financial concept each week

Learn Continuously

Invest in your financial education.

- Reading books about personal finance and money psychology
- Taking courses on budgeting, investing, or financial planning
- Listening to podcasts that discuss financial topics (that are not trying to sell you something)
- Attending workshops or seminars about money management

Practice Self-Compassion

Treat yourself kindly when you make financial mistakes.

- View mistakes as learning opportunities rather than personal failures.

- Remember that everyone struggles with financial decisions sometimes.
- Focus on progress rather than perfection.
- Celebrate small improvements in your financial habits.

Seek Support

Build relationships that support healthy financial development.

- Find friends who share your financial values.
- Consider working with a financial planner or counselor.
- Join groups focused on financial health and education.
- Seek mentorship from people who model healthy relationships with money.

The Freedom of Financial Identity Independence

When you successfully separate your worth from your wealth, you experience profound freedom that affects every area of your life.

Personal Freedom

There are personal benefits to feeling financially free.

Authentic Living: You can make choices based on your genuine preferences rather than what will impress others.

Risk-Taking: You can pursue opportunities and dreams without fearing that failure will diminish your worth as a person.

Creativity: You can explore interests and passions without needing them to be financially profitable.

Growth: You can learn and develop without needing to already be perfect or successful.

Peace: You can experience contentment regardless of your current financial circumstances.

Relational Freedom

There are relationship benefits to feeling financially free.

Genuine Connections: You can form authentic relationships based on mutual care rather than financial impressment.

Vulnerability: You can be honest about struggles and challenges without fearing judgment.

Generosity: You can give based on values and care rather than obligation or image management.

Boundaries: You can say no to social activities or expectations that don't serve your financial well-being.

Partnership: You can enter romantic relationships as an equal partner regardless of income differences.

Financial Freedom

There are practical benefits to feeling financially free.

Wise Decision-Making: You can make financial choices based on logic and values rather than insecurity and comparison.

Goal Clarity: You can set financial goals based on your actual needs and desires rather than external expectations.

Patience: You can build wealth gradually without needing to appear successful immediately.

Values Alignment: You can spend and save in ways that reflect your personal priorities.

Resilience: You can recover from financial setbacks without experiencing identity crises.

Exercises: Worth-Wealth Separation

Here are practical ways that you can help separate worth from wealth.

Weekly Identity Check-In

Every week, assess whether you're maintaining a healthy separation between worth and wealth.

Questions to Ask Yourself

- Did I make any financial decisions this week based on wanting to impress others?
- When did I feel most confident about myself? Was it related to money?

- What compliments or recognition did I receive? Were they financial or character-based?
- How did I respond to others' financial success or struggles?
- What am I grateful for this week that has nothing to do with money?

Values-Based Budgeting

Create a budget that reflects your actual values rather than societal expectations:

1. **Identify Your Core Values:** List the five to seven things that matter most to you in life.
2. **Assess Current Spending:** Review where your money actually goes.
3. **Align Spending with Values:** Adjust your budget to prioritize spending that supports what you truly care about.
4. **Eliminate Image Spending:** Reduce or eliminate spending that's primarily about appearing successful to others.
5. **Celebrate Alignment:** Take pride in financial choices that reflect your authentic priorities.

Gratitude Practice Beyond Money

Develop a daily gratitude practice that focuses on nonfinancial blessings.

Weekly Gratitude Categories

- **Monday:** Relationships and love
- **Tuesday:** Personal growth and learning
- **Wednesday:** Health and physical capabilities
- **Thursday:** Experiences and memories
- **Friday:** Personal qualities and character traits
- **Saturday:** Opportunities and potential
- **Sunday:** Ways you've contributed to others

Financial Anxiety Reality Check

When you notice financial anxiety, use this process to separate circumstance from identity.

1. **Name the Feeling:** "I'm feeling anxious about money."
2. **Identify the Trigger:** What specific situation caused the anxiety?
3. **Separate Fact from Story:** What is really true versus what story am I telling myself?
4. **Reaffirm Worth:** Remind yourself of your inherent value.
5. **Take Action:** What practical step can you take to address the situation?
6. **Release Control:** Acknowledge what aspects are beyond your control.

Look Forward: Money as a Tool, Not an Identity

Breaking the link between self-worth and money is not a one-time achievement but an ongoing practice. As you continue growing and changing throughout your lifetime, you'll face new challenges and opportunities that test this separation.

The goal isn't to stop caring about money or to avoid financial success. Money is a valuable tool that can provide security, opportunities, and the ability to contribute generously to causes you care about. The goal is to use money as a tool for creating the life you want rather than allowing it to determine your value as a person.

Money as Expression, Not Definition

When your worth is secure apart from wealth, money becomes a means of expressing your values rather than defining your identity.

- **Spending** reflects your priorities and brings joy without carrying identity weight.
- **Saving** demonstrates wisdom and planning without creating anxiety about worth.
- **Giving** flows from abundance and care rather than obligation or image management.
- **Earning** involves using your talents and skills without tying identity to salary levels.

- **Investing** becomes strategic planning rather than desperate attempts at wealth accumulation.

The Ripple Effects

People who successfully separate worth from wealth often find that this freedom positively impacts every area of their lives.

Career Choices: Making decisions based on fit, fulfillment, and long-term goals rather than just immediate salary.

Relationships: Forming deeper, more authentic connections based on mutual care and shared values.

Personal Growth: Taking healthy risks and pursuing learning opportunities without fear of failure.

Mental Health: Experiencing less anxiety, depression, and comparison-related stress.

Generosity: Being able to give time, money, and talents based on care rather than obligation.

Life Satisfaction: Finding genuine contentment that doesn't depend on external circumstances.

Your Worth Stands Alone

Your value as a human being was established long before you earned your first paycheck and will remain long after your final financial transaction. Your worth is not up for debate, not subject to market fluctuations and not dependent on others' approval or success.

In a culture that constantly tries to reduce you to your financial achievements, choosing to ground your identity in deeper truths is a radical act of self-love and wisdom. It's also a practical financial strategy—people who feel secure in their inherent worth make better financial decisions because they're not trying to prove their value through their purchases.

Whether you find your security in faith, in humanistic values, in relationships, or in personal growth, the key is recognizing that you are inherently valuable. Your money can fluctuate, your career can change, your possessions can be lost or gained, but your fundamental worth as a person remains constant.

This doesn't mean becoming passive about financial growth or abandoning ambition. It means pursuing financial goals from a place of security rather than desperation, making choices based on wisdom rather than fear and using money to express your values rather than establish your identity.

Don't confuse your work with your worth. Your value as a human being is not dependent upon what you own. This truth, fully embraced and consistently practiced, can transform not just your relationship with money but your entire approach to life. In a world that profits from your insecurity, recognizing your inherent worth is both revolutionary and liberating.

The journey toward separating self-worth from net worth is ongoing, but every step toward this freedom creates more space for authentic living, deeper relationships and genuine fulfillment. Your worth stands alone—secure, unchanging, and independent of any financial circumstance. From that foundation, you can build a financial life that serves your deepest values and highest aspirations.

Conclusion Chapter Eight

Don't confuse your work with your worth. Your value as a human being is not dependent upon what you own. Our pride can lead us to think that we need VIP status or a certain brand of consumer product. This can lead us to having credit card debt that we cannot afford to pay.

The next chapter is a more in-depth discussion about breaking poverty or scarcity thinking—that you will never have enough for what you really need.

CHAPTER 9

Breaking the Poverty Mindset

Many financial struggles stem from scarcity thinking—the belief that there may not won't be enough, because resources are or may be limited. This mindset creates a cycle of hoarding, anxiety, and competition that makes financial peace nearly impossible.

For young people today, the poverty mindset has been amplified by a new set of economic pressures—student loan debt that previous generations didn't face at this scale, housing costs that have outpaced income growth, job markets that demand more credentials for less security, and social media that constantly displays others' apparent abundance while highlighting your perceived lack.

Yet you also live in an era of unprecedented opportunity. Technology has democratized access to information, investment tools, and entrepreneurial possibilities. The global economy offers career flexibility that previous generations couldn't imagine. The challenge isn't lack of opportunity—it's recognizing abundance when scarcity thinking clouds your vision.

Breaking the poverty mindset doesn't mean ignoring real financial challenges or pretending that systemic economic problems don't exist. Instead, it means developing an abundance mindset that allows you to see opportunities, make wise decisions from a place of peace rather than panic, and build wealth through collaboration rather than competition.

Understand the Poverty Mindset

Poverty thinking operates like a lens that filters your perception of the world, making you focus on what's lacking rather than what's available. This lens was often formed during childhood through family experiences, cultural messages, or traumatic events, but it continues shaping your adult financial decisions in ways you might not consciously recognize.

Common Poverty Mindset Thoughts

Here are thoughts that almost everyone has—so you are not alone if you think this way from time to time.

Career Scarcity

- "There aren't enough good jobs for everyone."
- "I have to compete aggressively, or I'll be left behind."

- "If someone else gets promoted, it reduces my chances."
- "I need to hoard opportunities and connections."
- "Success in my field is only possible for a few lucky people."

Financial Scarcity

- "I'll never have enough money to feel secure."
- "Rich people took wealth away from everyone else."
- "If I spend money on enjoyment, I won't have enough for necessities."
- "I should buy things in bulk because I might not be able to afford them later."
- "Investing is too risky because I can't afford to lose anything."

Social Scarcity

- "If my friends succeed financially, it makes me look worse."
- "I can't afford to be generous because I need to protect what I have."
- "People only value relationships that benefit them financially."
- "I have to hide my financial struggles, or people will reject me."
- "There's not enough love/acceptance to go around."

Time and Energy Scarcity

- "I have to work constantly, or I'll fall behind."
- "There's not enough time to learn new skills or pursue opportunities."
- "I can't take breaks because someone else will get ahead."
- "Rest and enjoyment are luxuries I can't afford."
- "If I help others, I won't have enough energy for myself."

Consider NL, who works in marketing and constantly refreshes job boards, fearing her position isn't secure. She hoards vacation days because she's afraid to appear dispensable, works late every night to prove her value, and feels anxious when colleagues receive recognition. Her scarcity thinking makes her see every workplace interaction as competition rather than collaboration, actually limiting her career growth and job satisfaction.

The Origins of Poverty Mindset Thinking

Understanding where the poverty mindset comes from helps you recognize and change these patterns.

Family Financial Stress: Growing up in households where money was constantly a source of worry, argument, or deprivation can create lasting scarcity patterns. Even if your current circumstances are stable, you might carry anxiety from childhood financial insecurity.

Cultural Messages: Media, advertising, and social systems often profit from scarcity thinking. Messages like "limited time offer," "exclusive opportunity," and "only the best succeed" reinforce the belief that resources are scarce, and you must compete aggressively to get your share.

Economic Trauma: Experiencing job loss, economic recession, or financial crisis during formative years can create lasting poverty responses. If you graduated during the 2008 recession or started your career during the COVID-19 economic disruption, you might carry extra anxiety about financial security.

Social Comparison: Constant exposure to other people's financial highlight reels through social media creates artificial scarcity by making you feel like everyone else has more opportunities, money, or success than you do.

Educational Pressure: The message that you must constantly achieve and accumulate credentials to succeed creates pressure around learning, opportunity, and career advancement.

How Poverty Mindset Thinking Manifests in Daily Life

Poverty mindset affects your daily decisions and behaviors in ways you might not recognize.

Financial Behaviors

- Hoarding money in low-yield savings accounts because investing feels too risky

- Buying things you don't need because they're on sale or might not be available later
- Avoiding financial planning because thinking about the future feels overwhelming
- Working excessive hours because you fear not having enough income
- Refusing to spend money on experiences or items that would improve your quality of life

Career Behaviors

- Staying in unfulfilling jobs because you are afraid that better opportunities don't exist
- Avoiding networking because you see other professionals as competition
- Hoarding knowledge and skills instead of sharing them with colleagues
- Saying yes to every opportunity out of fear of missing out
- Avoiding career risks even when they could lead to better outcomes

Social Behaviors

- Comparing your financial situation to others and feeling inadequate
- Avoiding social activities because you're afraid you can't afford them

- Feeling threatened by friends' financial success instead of celebrating with them
- Being unable to be generous because you're focused on protecting what you have
- Isolating yourself when facing financial challenges instead of seeking support

Personal Development

- Avoiding learning new skills because you feel like you should already know everything
- Procrastinating on important goals because you're afraid of not having enough time or resources
- Focusing obsessively on what you lack rather than appreciating what you have
- Feeling like personal growth and financial success are either-or choices

The Cost of Living Under the Poverty Mindset

Poverty thinking doesn't just feel bad—it actively limits your financial growth and life satisfaction.

Financial Costs

Missed Opportunities: Poverty thinking makes you so focused on protecting what you have that you miss opportunities to grow your wealth. You might avoid investing, turn down career advancement opportunities, or refuse to start a business because you're afraid of losing what you currently have.

Poor Decision-Making: When you're operating from fear and scarcity, you make reactive decisions instead of strategic ones. You might take the first job offer you receive instead of negotiating or exploring better options. You might avoid necessary spending that would improve your earning potential.

Relationship Damage: Poverty thinking damages relationships that could provide career opportunities, emotional support, or collaborative ventures. When you see others as competitors rather than potential partners, you limit your access to networks that could benefit everyone involved.

Energy Depletion: Constantly worrying about not having enough is mentally and emotionally exhausting. This depletion reduces your ability to be creative, productive, and strategic about building wealth.

Consider MJ, who has twenty-five thousand dollars in a savings account earning 0.1 percent interest because he's afraid of losing money in investments. His poverty thinking is actually guaranteeing that inflation will erode his purchasing power over time. Meanwhile, he continues working a job he dislikes because he's afraid to risk changing careers, even though his skills could command a higher salary in a different company.

Emotional and Mental Health Costs

Chronic Anxiety: Poverty thinking creates constant low-level anxiety about the future. You worry about running out of money, missing opportunities, or being left behind. This anxiety affects sleep, relationships, and overall life satisfaction.

Depression and Hopelessness: When you believe resources are limited, and you're in constant competition with others, it's easy to feel hopeless about improving your situation. This can lead to depression and a sense of powerlessness.

Relationship Difficulties: Scarcity thinking makes you suspicious of others' motives, envious of their success, and protective of your resources. This damages friendships, romantic relationships, and family connections.

Perfectionism and Control Issues: If you believe there isn't enough to go around, you might try to control every aspect of your financial life, leading to perfectionism that prevents action and growth.

Career and Professional Costs

Poverty thinking creates obstacles that you don't need in your life and it can expensive and wasteful.

Limited Growth: Poverty thinking makes you focus on protecting your current position rather than growing into new opportunities. You might avoid taking on challenging projects, seeking promotions, or changing companies.

Poor Networking: When you see other professionals as competition rather than potential collaborators, you limit your professional network and miss opportunities for mutual support and advancement.

Innovation Resistance: Poverty thinking makes you risk-averse, preventing you from developing new skills, trying innovative approaches, or pursuing entrepreneurial ventures.

Burnout: The belief that you must work constantly to protect your position leads to overwork and burnout, ultimately reducing your productivity and career satisfaction.

The Abundance Alternative

The antidote to poverty thinking isn't denial of real financial challenges or naive optimism. Instead, it's developing what researchers call an *abundance mindset*—the belief that there are enough resources for you. Also, that there are opportunities for everyone to succeed, and that success doesn't have to come at others' expense.

Core Principles of Abundance Thinking

In contrast to poverty thinking, abundance thinking is that there will be enough, somehow, some way.

Expansion Versus Competition: Abundance thinking recognizes that wealth and opportunity can be created, not just redistributed. When you help others succeed, you often create opportunities for your own success as well.

Collaboration Versus Competition: Instead of seeing others as competitors, abundance thinking recognizes that collaboration often leads to better outcomes for everyone involved.

Growth Versus Protection: Rather than focusing primarily on protecting what you have, abundance thinking emphasizes growing and developing new resources and opportunities.

Possibility Versus Limitation: Abundance thinking focuses on what's possible rather than what's lacking, leading to more creative problem-solving and opportunity recognition.

Gratitude Versus Complaint: Instead of focusing on what you don't have, abundance thinking starts with appreciating what you do have and building from there.

Abundance Thinking in Practice

What does abundance thinking sound like to our inner voice?

Career Abundance

- "There are multiple paths to success in my field."
- "Helping colleagues succeed creates opportunities for everyone."
- "My skills and talents can create value in various situations."
- "Challenges are opportunities to learn and grow."
- "The economy constantly creates new opportunities."

Financial Abundance

- "Money is a tool that can be earned, saved, and grown through wise decisions."
- "There are multiple ways to build wealth and financial security."
- "Investing allows me to participate in economic growth."
- "Generosity and financial growth can happen simultaneously."
- "Financial setbacks are temporary and can be learning experiences."

Social Abundance

- "Others' success doesn't diminish my opportunities."
- "Relationships are sources of mutual support and growth."
- "I can be generous because there's enough love and resources to share."
- "Communities become stronger when everyone contributes."
- "Collaboration creates opportunities that wouldn't exist individually."

Strategies for Breaking the Poverty Mindset

Shifting from poverty to abundance thinking requires intentional practice and specific strategies.

Daily Abundance Practices

Gratitude Inventory: Start each day by listing three things you're grateful for that aren't financial. This trains your brain to notice abundance in your current situation.

- Relationships that support and encourage you
- Skills and talents you possess
- Experiences that have enriched your life
- Health and physical capabilities
- Opportunities available to you today

Possibility Journaling: Each evening, write about one opportunity you noticed during the day or one way you could approach a challenge differently. This develops your ability to see possibilities rather than just problems.

Abundance Affirmations: Replace scarcity thoughts with abundance statements.

- Instead of "I can't afford this," try "I'm choosing to spend my money differently."
- Instead of "There aren't enough opportunities," try "I'm open to discovering new opportunities."
- Instead of "I'm behind everyone else," try "I'm on my own unique path."

- Instead of "I might lose everything," try "I'm building skills and relationships that create security."

Financial Abundance Strategies

What can you do? Here are practical steps.

Investment Mindset: Instead of only protecting money through savings, develop an investment mindset that allows money to grow.

- Start small with index funds or other diversified investments.
- Learn about compound interest and how time amplifies investment growth.
- Recognize that some risk is necessary for financial growth.
- View market fluctuations as normal rather than threatening.

Skills Investment: Invest in developing skills that increase your earning potential.

- Take courses that enhance your career prospects.
- Learn new technologies or methodologies in your field.
- Develop communication and leadership skills.
- Build expertise that makes you valuable in multiple contexts.

Network Building: Approach networking from an abundance mindset.

- Focus on how you can help others rather than just what they can do for you.
- Build relationships based on mutual interest and support.
- Share knowledge and resources generously.
- Celebrate others' successes genuinely.

Consider NO, who shifted from scarcity to abundance thinking about her marketing career. Instead of hoarding client contacts and competing with colleagues, she started sharing resources, collaborating on projects, and celebrating team successes. This approach led to stronger relationships, better project outcomes, and ultimately a promotion because her collaborative approach made her valuable to the organization.

Career Abundance Approaches

Mindset thinking also affects your work life. Here are ideas.

Growth Mindset: Adopt beliefs that support career development.

- View challenges as opportunities to develop new capabilities.
- See feedback as information for improvement rather than criticism.
- Recognize that skills can be developed through effort and learning.
- Focus on progress rather than comparing yourself to others.

Opportunity Creation: Instead of waiting for opportunities to appear, create them.

- Volunteer for projects that develop new skills.
- Propose solutions to problems you notice in your workplace.
- Seek mentorship relationships with people you admire.
- Start side projects that explore your interests and capabilities.

Value Creation: Focus on creating value rather than just protecting your position.

- Look for ways to improve processes or solve problems.
- Develop expertise that benefits your entire team or organization.
- Share knowledge and skills that help others succeed.
- Take initiative on projects that align with your strengths.

Social Abundance Practices

Generous Mindset: Practice generosity even when resources feel limited.

- Give your time and attention to causes you care about.
- Share knowledge and skills with others.
- Offer emotional support to friends and family.

- Contribute to your community in ways that match your resources.

Celebration Practice: Genuinely celebrate others' successes.

- Share friends' achievements on social media.
- Express genuine happiness when colleagues receive recognition.
- Ask about others' goals and support their efforts.
- View others' success as evidence that success is possible.

Support Seeking: Ask for help when you need it, recognizing that community support is abundant when you participate authentically.

- Join professional organizations or networking groups.
- Seek mentorship from people whose careers you admire.
- Participate in communities related to your interests and goals.
- Be vulnerable about the challenges you're facing.

Faith Perspectives on Abundance vs. Scarcity

Your worldview significantly influences your relationship with abundance and scarcity.

Faith-Based Abundance

Scripture consistently presents God as abundant and generous, providing multiple perspectives on overcoming poverty mindset thinking.

God's Provision: "God will meet all your needs according to the riches of his glory in Christ Jesus" (Philippians 4:19). This doesn't promise wealth, but it assures that God's resources are sufficient for your actual needs.

Generous Nature: "Every good and perfect gift is from above, coming down from the Father of the heavenly lights" (James 1:17). Recognition that good things come from God's generous nature rather than from scarcity-driven competition.

Faith Economics: Jesus taught principles that directly contradict scarcity thinking:

- "Give and it will be given to you" (Luke 6:38).
- "Whoever desires to save his life will lose it, but whoever loses their life for My sake will find it" (Matthew 16:25) NKJV.
- The parable of talents emphasizes multiplication through wise stewardship rather than fearful hoarding.

Community Abundance: The early church modeled abundance thinking through radical generosity and mutual support: "All the believers were together and had everything in common" (Acts 2:44).

Consider WK, who struggled with financial anxiety despite having stable employment. Through studying biblical principles about God's provision and participating in a church small group focused on financial stewardship, he learned to view money as a tool for service rather than security. This shift allowed him to be more generous, take healthy career risks and experience greater peace about his financial future.

Abundance Thinking:

Regular practices for those with an abundance mindset:

- **Prayer and Trust:** Regularly pray about financial concerns and practice trusting God's provision.
- **Tithing and Generosity:** Give consistently as an expression of abundance faith.
- **Community Support:** Participate in communities that provide mutual support and encouragement.
- **Service Focus:** Use money and skills to serve others based on your values and priorities.
- **Eternal Perspective:** Remember that earthly wealth is temporary and ultimate security comes from relationship with God.

Abundance

There are various types of abundance.

Economic Abundance: Understanding that economies grow through innovation, collaboration and value creation helps counter zero-sum thinking:

- Economic history shows consistent long-term growth driven by human creativity and innovation.
- Technological advancement continues creating new opportunities and industries.
- Global connectivity provides access to markets and opportunities that didn't exist for previous generations.

Social Abundance: Recognizing that human cooperation and community support create abundance for everyone:

- Strong communities benefit all members through mutual support and resource sharing.
- Diverse networks provide access to opportunities, knowledge and collaboration.
- Social movements and collective action can create positive change that benefits many people.

Personal Abundance: Developing confidence in your own capacity for growth and contribution:

- Neuroplasticity research shows that brains continue developing throughout life.
- Skill development and learning can continue indefinitely.
- Personal resilience can be developed through practice and experience.
- Individual creativity and problem-solving can create value and opportunities.

Philosophical Abundance: Many philosophical traditions emphasize abundance and interconnection:

- Humanism emphasizes human potential and the capacity for positive change.
- Systems thinking recognizes how individual success connects to community well-being.
- Mindfulness practices help you appreciate present abundance rather than focus on future scarcity.

Consider BR, works in technology. She initially struggled with imposter syndrome and fear that her success was taking opportunities away from others. Through reading about economic growth, participating in mentorship programs and practicing mindfulness, she learned to view the tech industry as constantly expanding rather than zero-sum. This mindset shift allowed her to pursue leadership opportunities and mentor other women in tech.

Strategies for Abundance Thinking:

Practical steps to achieve an abundance mindset:

- **Education and Learning:** Continuously develop knowledge and skills that create value.
- **Community Engagement:** Participate in communities focused on mutual support and growth.
- **Mindfulness Practice:** Develop present-moment awareness that helps you notice current abundance.
- **Systems Thinking:** Understand how individual success connects to broader social and economic health.

- **Historical Perspective:** Study how human innovation and cooperation have consistently created abundance over time.

Overcome Specific Poverty Mindset Triggers

Certain situations commonly trigger poverty mindset thinking. Recognizing and preparing for these triggers helps maintain abundance mindset.

Financial Setbacks and Uncertainty

Obstacles can affect us all; The following are example situations and what you may want to consider.

Common Triggers:

- Job loss or income reduction.
- Unexpected expenses like medical bills or car repairs.
- Market downturns that affect investments.
- Comparison with peers who appear more financially successful.
- Economic news that emphasizes recession or financial crisis.

Abundance Responses:

- View setbacks as temporary situations rather than permanent conditions.
- Focus on skills, relationships and knowledge that can't be lost.

- Look for opportunities that might arise from challenging circumstances.
- Seek support from community rather than isolating in shame.
- Remember past challenges you've successfully navigated.

Steps:

- Build emergency funds gradually to create actual financial security.
- Develop multiple income streams to reduce dependence on single sources.
- Maintain professional networks that can provide support during transitions.
- Continue learning and skill development even during stable periods.
- Practice gratitude for what remains stable during uncertain times.

Career Competition and Comparison

Here are thoughts that can create obstacles but you can overcome them.

Common Triggers:

- Colleagues receiving promotions or recognition.
- Industry changes that threaten job security.
- Social media posts about others' career achievements.

- Job searching in competitive markets.
- Performance reviews or workplace evaluations.

Abundance Responses:

- View others' success as evidence that advancement is possible.
- Focus on developing unique value rather than competing directly.
- Build collaborative relationships rather than viewing colleagues as threats.
- Celebrate others' achievements genuinely.
- Define success personally rather than accepting external definitions.

Steps:

- Set personal development goals independent of others' progress.
- Seek mentorship relationships that provide guidance and perspective.
- Practice skills sharing and collaboration with colleagues.
- Build expertise in areas that align with your interests and strengths.
- Focus on long-term career development rather than short-term competition.

Social and Lifestyle Pressure

Don't be surprised if you experience these kinds of obstacles. Just don't let them get in your way.

Common Triggers:

- Friends' lifestyle choices that seem more expensive than you can afford.
- Social media posts showing experiences or possessions you can't afford.
- Family expectations about financial milestones.
- Dating and relationship pressure related to financial stability.
- Cultural messages about success and achievement.

Abundance Responses:

- Remember that everyone has different financial circumstances and priorities.
- Focus on relationships and experiences that don't require significant spending.
- Define lifestyle success according to your values rather than external expectations.
- Practice gratitude for the experiences and relationships you do have.
- Recognize that social media presentations rarely reflect complete reality.

Steps:

- Set social spending budgets that align with your financial goals.
- Communicate honestly with friends about your financial boundaries.
- Find low-cost activities and experiences that bring you joy.
- Limit social media consumption when it triggers comparison and scarcity feelings.
- Build relationships based on shared interests rather than shared spending capacity.

Build Long-Term Abundance Habits

Creating lasting change in your relationship with poverty and abundance requires developing consistent habits and practices.

Daily Abundance Rituals

Regular practices can be very effective.

Morning Abundance Practice:

- Begin each day with gratitude for three nonfinancial blessings.
- Set intentions for how you want to approach opportunities and challenges.
- Review your goals and visualize positive outcomes.
- Affirm your belief in abundance and possibility.

Evening Reflection:

- Identify one opportunity you noticed during the day.
- Acknowledge one way you contributed positively to others.
- Appreciate one skill or capability you used effectively.
- Plan one small step toward a goal for tomorrow.

Weekly Abundance Review:

- Assess your spending and financial decisions for abundance vs. scarcity motivation.
- Celebrate financial progress and learning, however small.
- Identify opportunities for generosity or collaboration.
- Plan activities and experiences that bring joy without requiring significant spending.

Monthly Growth Practices

Try these about once a month.

Skills Investment:

- Spend time each month learning something new related to your career or interests.
- Practice skills that increase your value in professional or personal contexts.
- Seek feedback from mentors, colleagues, or friends about areas for development.

- Set learning goals that expand your capabilities and opportunities.

Network Development:

- Reach out to one new professional contact each month.
- Maintain relationships with existing network through regular communication.
- Look for ways to help others in your network achieve their goals.
- Participate in professional or community organizations.

Financial Growth:

- Review and adjust investment contributions.
- Assess financial goals and celebrate progress.
- Learn about new financial strategies or tools.
- Practice generosity within your financial capacity.

Annual Abundance Assessment

About once a year, when you are not under extreme pressure, I suggest that you do these. Perhaps do not do them during times of the year when you are busier or more pressed with other activities. For example, if income tax preparation time makes you feel stressed out, do this a different time. Adjust it for your own situation.

Values Alignment Review:

- Assess whether your financial decisions align with your stated values.
- Identify areas where poverty thinking might be limiting your growth.
- Set goals for the coming year that reflect abundance mindset.
- Plan experiences and activities that support your well-being and growth.

Goal-Setting and Vision:

- Create financial goals that reflect abundance thinking.
- Set career objectives that focus on contribution and growth rather than just protection.
- Plan ways to contribute to your community and support others.
- Envision the kind of impact you want to make in the world.

The Ripple Effects of Abundance Thinking

When you successfully break the scarcity spell, the effects extend far beyond your personal finances.

Personal Benefits

I want to encourage you to know that you will feel better with abundance thinking.

Increased Creativity: Abundance thinking frees mental and emotional energy for creative problem-solving and innovation.

Better Decision-Making: When you're not operating from fear, you can make strategic decisions based on long-term thinking rather than reactive choices.

Improved Mental Health: Abundance thinking reduces anxiety, increases optimism and promotes overall psychological well-being.

Enhanced Relationships: When you're not competing with everyone, you can form deeper, more authentic connections based on mutual support.

Greater Life Satisfaction: Focusing on abundance and possibility leads to increased contentment and appreciation for your life circumstances.

Professional Benefits

Career Growth: Abundance thinking promotes risk-taking, collaboration and innovation that lead to professional advancement.

Leadership Development: People with abundance mindsets often become natural leaders because they focus on creating value for everyone.

Network Expansion: Collaborative approaches to professional relationships build stronger, more supportive networks.

Entrepreneurial Success: Abundance thinking provides the optimism and possibility focus necessary for successful business ventures.

Social Benefits

Community Building: Abundance-minded individuals often become catalysts for positive community development and social change.

Generous Impact: When you believe that you will have enough and that there's enough to go around, you're more likely to contribute generously to causes and people you care about.

Positive Influence: Your abundance mindset influences others to adopt similar approaches, creating positive ripple effects.

Cultural Change: As more individuals adopt abundance thinking, it contributes to cultural shifts away from zero-sum competition toward collaborative growth.

Break Free from the Spell

The poverty mindset spell is powerful because it feels protective—it seems to keep you safe by making you constantly vigilant about potential threats to your resources and security. But this protection comes at enormous cost: it limits your growth, damages your relationships and prevents you from experiencing the joy and possibility that life offers.

Breaking this spell doesn't mean ignoring real challenges or pretending that systemic problems don't exist. We do face economic pressures that create legitimate concerns about financial security. The difference is responding to these challenges from a place of abundance rather than scarcity.

When you operate from abundance, you see challenges as problems to be solved rather than evidence that you're doomed to struggle. You view others' success as inspiration rather than threat. You make financial decisions based on long-term strategy rather than short-term fear. You build wealth through value creation and collaboration rather than hoarding and competition.

This mindset shift isn't always easy, especially when life experiences, cultural messages, economic pressures, life and social media constantly reinforce poverty mindset thinking. But every time you choose abundance over scarcity—every time you celebrate a friend's success, take a calculated risk, invest in your future, or give generously—you weaken the spell's hold on your life.

The abundance alternative recognizes that you will have enough, that there are enough resources and opportunities for everyone to succeed, that success doesn't have to come at others' expense and that wealth and opportunity can be created through wisdom, collaboration and contribution. This mindset opens up possibilities that scarcity thinking closes off, creates opportunities that competition destroys and builds wealth that hoarding prevents.

Young people have unprecedented access to information, tools and opportunities—along with facing unprecedented challenges and pressures. Whether you experience this environment as abundant or scarce depends largely on the lens through which you view it. Breaking the poverty mindset spell allows you to see and seize the abundance that surrounds you while building financial and personal wealth that serves not just yourself but your entire community.

The spell of poverty mindset is real, but it's not permanent. With faith, intentional practice, community support and commitment to abundance thinking, you can break free from its limitations and step into the financial and personal freedom that abundance offers. The world needs people who believe in possibility, who create value through collaboration and who build wealth through wisdom rather than fear. Breaking the scarcity spell is your first step toward becoming one of them

Conclusion Chapter Nine

Many financial struggles stem from poverty mindset thinking—the belief that you won't have enough, that there isn't enough to go around, that resources are limited and that someone else's gain means your loss. This mindset creates a cycle of hoarding, anxiety and competition that makes financial peace nearly impossible.

Poverty mindset thinking shows up in various ways:

- Buying in bulk or hoarding supplies because you're afraid of running out.
- Avoiding investments because you're afraid of losing what you have.
- Working excessive hours because you're afraid of not having enough.

- Competing with others rather than collaborating.
- Focusing on what you lack rather than what you have.

The antidote to poverty mindset thinking isn't denial of real financial challenges or naive optimism. Instead, it's developing what researchers call an "abundance mindset"—the belief that you will have what you need, that there are enough resources and opportunities for everyone to succeed and that success doesn't have to come at others' expense.

This mindset shift opens up possibilities that scarcity thinking closes off. Instead of hoarding, you can be generous. Instead of competing, you can collaborate. Instead of focusing on limitations, you can focus on opportunities. You can follow your life's purpose.

CHAPTER 10

The Gratitude Revolution

Perhaps no single practice is more transformative for your money identity than developing genuine gratitude for what you already have. Gratitude isn't just a spiritual blessing or feel-good emotion—it's a powerful financial tool that can literally rewire your brain's response to money and possessions. Having a grateful mindset impacts the chemicals in your brain like dopamine, serotonin and oxytocin—which give you a sense of peace.

Navigating financial stress, career uncertainty and constant social comparison, gratitude might seem impossible or even naive. When you're struggling with student loans, worried about job security, or watching peers seemingly succeed faster than you are, the suggestion to "just be grateful" can feel dismissive of real challenges.

But true gratitude isn't about denying problems or pretending everything is perfect. It's about developing the ability to simultaneously acknowledge challenges while recognizing the abundance that already exists in your life. This revolutionary shift in perspective transforms not just how you feel about money, but how you make financial decisions, relate to others and build lasting wealth.

The Science of Gratitude and Money

Research in neuroscience and psychology reveals that gratitude creates measurable changes in brain function and behavior that directly impact financial decision-making.

Neurological Changes

When you practice gratitude regularly, your brain undergoes structural changes that affect how you perceive and respond to financial situations:

Increased Dopamine Production: Gratitude activates the brain's reward system, producing dopamine—the same neurotransmitter involved in addiction and pleasure-seeking. When you feel genuinely grateful, you experience satisfaction without needing to purchase anything.

Enhanced Serotonin Levels: Gratitude increases serotonin production, which regulates mood and promotes feelings of well-being. Higher serotonin levels reduce the likelihood of emotional spending and impulse purchases.

Oxytocin Release: Often called the "bonding hormone," oxytocin is released during gratitude practices.

This promotes connection and reduces the isolation that often drives compensatory spending.

Prefrontal Cortex Strengthening: Regular gratitude practice strengthens the prefrontal cortex—the brain region responsible for executive function, impulse control and long-term planning. This directly improves financial decision-making capabilities.

Stress Hormone Reduction: Gratitude reduces cortisol production. Lower stress levels lead to better sleep, clearer thinking and less reactive financial decisions.

Consider EM, who started a daily gratitude practice after recognizing that financial stress was affecting her sleep and relationships. Within two months, she noticed that she no longer felt compelled to shop when stressed, was more patient with financial planning and felt more optimistic about her financial future. Her gratitude practice didn't change her income, but it transformed her relationship with money.

Behavioral Changes

Gratitude practice creates specific behavioral changes that improve financial outcomes:

Reduced Hedonic Adaptation: Gratitude helps you continue appreciating purchases and experiences rather than quickly adapting to them and needing more stimulation.

Improved Impulse Control: People who practice gratitude show better self-control in laboratory tests, including the ability to delay gratification for better long-term outcomes and lasting gratification.

Enhanced Social Connection: Grateful people build stronger relationships, which often provide financial benefits through networking, support and collaboration opportunities.

Increased Generosity: Gratitude promotes generous behavior, which paradoxically often leads to increased financial opportunities and life satisfaction.

Better Decision-Making: Grateful individuals make more thoughtful, less reactive decisions in all areas of life, including finances.

The Gratitude Deficit in Culture

Challenges make gratitude particularly difficult but also particularly necessary.

Cultural Gratitude Barriers Include:

Comparison Culture: Social media creates constant opportunities to compare your life to others' financial highlight reels, making it difficult to appreciate your own circumstances.

Achievement Pressure: Messages about needing to constantly achieve, improve and advance make it hard to appreciate current accomplishments and circumstances.

Consumer Messaging: Advertising specifically targets dissatisfaction, constantly suggesting that you need more to be happy, successful, or worthy.

Economic Anxiety: Legitimate concerns about student debt, housing costs and job security make it challenging to feel grateful for financial circumstances.

Instant Gratification Culture: Apps, services and technologies designed for immediate satisfaction make it harder to appreciate gradual progress and long-term benefits. Lasting gratification is better.

Individual Success Mythology: Cultural emphasis on individual achievement can prevent recognition of the support systems, opportunities and advantages that contribute to success.

The Complaint Culture Problem

Complaining, on the other hand, is a waste of time because it doesn't change anything and it won't make you feel better. It affects cortisol, a stress hormone which is linked to risk of heart disease, high cholesterol, diabetes, obesity, strokes, a weakened immune system. It can affect how your brain works, as the negative thought patterns affect the part of your brain used for problem-solving and cognitive functions. It also has negative effects on those around you.

Consider TY, who works in a corporate job he finds unfulfilling. He regularly complains to friends about his work, his salary and his career prospects. This complaint pattern reinforces his dissatisfaction, prevents him from seeing opportunities for improvement and affects his relationships with colleagues and friends. His constant focus on what's wrong keeps him stuck in patterns that prevent positive change.

The Physiology of Complaining:

Here are reasons to stop complaining:

Increased Cortisol: Chronic complaining keeps your stress response system activated, leading to anxiety, poor sleep and impaired decision-making.

Neural Pathway Reinforcement: Complaining strengthens neural pathways associated with negative thinking, making it easier to see problems and harder to notice opportunities.

Social Isolation: Chronic complainers often find that others avoid spending time with them, reducing social support and networking opportunities.

Reduced Problem-Solving: Focusing on problems without seeking solutions actually impairs your ability to find creative alternatives and improvements.

Victim Mindset Reinforcement: Constant complaining reinforces feelings of powerlessness and external control, preventing proactive behavior change.

First-World Problems and Perspective

Don't be concerned with "first-world problems." Did your vacation not go as well as you hoped? Did you lose power for your cell phone or TV set overnight? Was the meal you ate at that restaurant not fabulous?

Understanding the privilege you have in the world helps maintain perspective. The lifestyle most of us have in America was unimaginable during biblical times and is considered to be extremely wealthy in most parts of the world.

This perspective isn't about dismissing legitimate concerns or feeling guilty about your circumstances. Instead, it's about recognizing that many things you might take for granted represent abundance that most humans throughout history couldn't even imagine.

Global Perspective Benefits:

Here is one time that I think it may actually help to compare yourself. How does your lifestyle compare to the tens of millions of people (about one out of every ten of us) who live on less than three dollars per day, which is the international measure for people who live in extreme poverty.

Reduced Trivial Stress: Recognizing that many daily frustrations are minor in the context of global human experience reduces their emotional impact.

Increased Appreciation: Understanding how privileged many aspects of your life are increases genuine appreciation for them.

Problem Prioritization: Global perspective helps you focus energy on problems that actually matter rather than minor inconveniences.

Generous Motivation: Awareness of global needs often motivates generous action that benefits both recipients and givers.

Resilience Building: Understanding that you can handle minor difficulties builds confidence for facing more significant challenges.

Develop a Revolutionary Gratitude Practice

Effective gratitude practice goes beyond occasional thankfulness or positive thinking. It involves developing specific habits and perspectives that consistently shift your attention toward abundance.

Daily Gratitude Fundamentals

Here are suggestions of habits to experience gratitude:

Morning Gratitude Inventory: Begin each day by identifying specific things you're grateful for:

Categories for Daily Practice:

- **Physical Health:** Body functions, abilities, energy levels.
- **Relationships:** People who love, support, or encourage you.
- **Opportunities:** Education, career, personal growth possibilities.
- **Basic Needs:** Housing, food, safety, healthcare access.
- **Experiences:** Memories, learning, beauty you've encountered.

- **Personal Qualities:** Strengths, skills, character traits you possess.
- **Future Possibilities:** Dreams, goals, potential outcomes you anticipate.

Gratitude Journaling Techniques:

The Three Good Things: Each evening, write about three positive things that happened during the day and why you think they occurred.

Gratitude Letters: Monthly, write detailed letters to people who have positively impacted your life, expressing specific appreciation for their influence.

Gratitude Photography: Take daily photos of things you're grateful for, creating a visual record of abundance in your life.

Financial Gratitude Specific: Weekly, identify three financial blessings, however small—a paycheck, the ability to buy coffee, having savings, paying bills on time.

Advanced Gratitude Practices

Once you have the previous suggestions mastered, go even deeper for more meaningful results.

Gratitude in Difficulty: Practice finding things to be grateful for even during challenging circumstances:

Job Search Gratitude: If unemployed, appreciate having time to explore options, skills that make you employable, people supporting your search, or the opportunity to reassess career direction.

Debt Gratitude: If carrying debt, appreciate the education, experiences, or necessities the debt provided, your ability to make payments, or the learning opportunities debt management provides.

Relationship Difficulty Gratitude: During conflicts, appreciate what you've learned about yourself, the other person's positive qualities, or growth opportunities the situation provides.

Be thankful "in" all circumstances. This does not mean be thankful "for" all circumstances.

This distinction is crucial: you don't have to feel grateful that difficult things happen, but you can find things to be grateful for even while difficult things are occurring.

Consider CR, who was laid off from her engineering job. Instead of only focusing on the financial stress and job search challenges, she practiced finding gratitude within the situation: appreciation for severance pay that provided transition time, the opportunity to reassess her career goals, supportive friends and family and the chance to develop resilience. This gratitude practice didn't eliminate her challenges, but it prevented them from overwhelming her and helped her maintain the positive attitude that ultimately contributed to finding a better position.

Social and Financial Gratitude Integration

For deeper level of gratitude put it all together.

Gratitude-Based Spending: Make purchasing decisions from a place of appreciation rather than deprivation:

Before Purchases: Ask yourself, "Am I buying this from gratitude for what I already have, or from dissatisfaction with what I lack?"

After Purchases: Practice appreciating items that you buy rather than immediately focusing on the next thing you want.

Experience Gratitude: When spending on experiences, fully appreciate them while they're happening rather than just documenting them for social media.

Service Gratitude: When paying for services, appreciate the people providing them and the convenience they offer.

Gratitude-Based Generosity: Give money and time from appreciation rather than obligation.

Abundance-Based Giving: Give because you appreciate what you have rather than because you feel guilty about having more than others.

Skill Sharing: Share your talents and knowledge as expressions of gratitude for the opportunities you've had to develop them.

Time Generosity: Volunteer your time appreciating the opportunity to contribute rather than viewing service as sacrifice.

Relationship Investment: Spend money on relationships from gratitude for the people in your life rather than from social obligation.

Faith-Based Gratitude Approaches

Your spiritual or philosophical worldview significantly influences how you approach gratitude practice.

Gratitude

Scripture presents gratitude not just as a positive emotion but as a fundamental response to God's character and provision.

Gratitude as Worship: "Give thanks to the Lord, for he is good, his love endures forever" (Psalm 107:1). Gratitude becomes a way of acknowledging God's goodness and faithfulness.

Gratitude in All Circumstances: "Rejoice always, pray continually, give thanks in all circumstances; for this is the will of God for you in Christ Jesus" (1 Thessalonians 5:16-18). This doesn't mean being happy about everything, but finding reasons for thanksgiving even during difficulties.

Gratitude for Provision: "God will meet all of needs according to the riches of his glory in Christ Jesus" (Philippians 4:19). Recognizing that God provides what you need creates gratitude that reduces financial anxiety.

Gratitude for Grace: "God, who is rich in mercy, made us alive with Christ even when we were dead in transgressions—it is by grace you have been saved" (Ephesians 2:4-5). Ultimate gratitude comes from recognizing undeserved love and salvation.

Gratitude Practices

Prayer-Based Gratitude: Include thanksgiving in daily prayers, specifically acknowledging God's provision and faithfulness.

Scripture Meditation: Study biblical passages about God's faithfulness and provision, allowing them to increase appreciation for His care.

Community Gratitude: Share testimonies of God's provision with other believers, building faith and encouraging others.

Service Gratitude: Serve others as expressions of gratitude for what God has done in your life.

Stewardship Gratitude: Manage money as an expression of gratitude for God's provision rather than anxiety about security.

Consider MM, who struggled with financial anxiety despite having steady employment. Through studying biblical passages about God's provision and practicing daily gratitude prayers, he learned to see his job, health, and relationships as gifts from God rather than things he had to protect through anxious effort. This shift reduced his financial stress and increased his generosity and contentment.

Other Types of Gratitude

If you don't identify as religious, gratitude can still be a powerful practice grounded in humanistic, philosophical, or scientific principles.

Humanistic Gratitude

Appreciation for human connection, achievement, and potential can look like the following:

Gratitude for the people who have contributed to your development and opportunities

Appreciation for human creativity, innovation, and progress that benefit your life

Recognition of your own potential and capacity for growth and contribution

Scientific Gratitude

Appreciation based on understanding natural processes and interconnection can manifest as the following:

- Gratitude for the complexity and beauty of natural systems that support life
- Appreciation for scientific knowledge that improves health, communication, and quality of life
- Recognition of your place in larger ecological and social systems

Philosophical Gratitude

Appreciation based on meaning-making and values can show up in ways like the following:

- Gratitude for the opportunity to create meaning and purpose in your life
- Appreciation for beauty, art, literature, and culture that enrich human experience

- Recognition of your ability to make positive contributions to others and society

Social Gratitude

Appreciation for community and mutual support can be expressed in the following ways:

- Gratitude for relationships that provide love, support, and growth opportunities
- Appreciation for social systems and institutions that provide security and opportunity
- Recognition of interdependence and mutual benefit in human communities

Secular Gratitude Practices

Here are other suggestions about achieving gratitude.

Nature-Based Gratitude: Spend time in natural settings appreciating the complexity and beauty of ecological systems.

Art and Culture Gratitude: Regularly appreciate music, literature, visual art, and cultural expressions that enrich your life.

Relationship Gratitude: Actively appreciate the people in your life and express that appreciation regularly.

Achievement Gratitude: Acknowledge your own accomplishments and the people and circumstances that made them possible.

Learning Gratitude: Appreciate opportunities to learn, grow, and develop throughout your life.

Consider KF, who works as an environmental scientist. She developed a gratitude practice based on appreciation for natural systems, scientific discovery, and human cooperation in addressing environmental challenges. This practice helped her maintain optimism about her career impact and reduced stress about her modest nonprofit salary by focusing on the meaningful contribution her work represents.

Financial Applications of Gratitude

Gratitude becomes most powerful when it directly influences your financial decisions and behaviors.

Gratitude-Based Budgeting

Create budgets that reflect appreciation for what you have rather than anxiety about what you lack.

Abundance Categories

Include budget categories for things you're grateful to afford.

- "Relationship Investment" for money spent on friends and family
- "Health Gratitude" for healthcare, fitness, and wellness expenses
- "Growth Investment" for education, books, courses, and skill development
- "Beauty Appreciation" for art, music, entertainment, and aesthetic experiences

- "Service Gratitude" for charitable giving and community contribution

Gratitude Before Spending

Before major purchases, practice gratitude for the following:

- The income that makes the purchase possible
- Existing possessions that serve similar functions
- The people and systems that create the products or services you're buying
- The opportunity to make choices about how to spend money

Spending Review Gratitude

Weekly, review your spending with appreciation.

- Appreciate bills you can pay rather than resenting them.
- Be grateful for the services and products you purchased rather than immediately wanting more.
- Acknowledge the work and effort that created your income.
- Appreciate the freedom to make spending choices.

Investment and Saving Through Gratitude

Make gratitude work for you financially.

Gratitude-Based Investment

Invest from appreciation rather than fear.

- Appreciate the opportunity to participate in economic growth.
- Be grateful for companies and innovations that create value.
- Recognize investing as a form of optimism about human creativity and progress.
- Appreciate the profound benefits of compound interest and time-based wealth building.

Savings Appreciation

Find gratitude in saving money.

- Appreciate the security that emergency funds provide.
- Be grateful for the self-control that enables saving.
- Recognize savings as future opportunities rather than current deprivation.
- Appreciate the peace of mind that financial reserves create.

Debt Management Gratitude

Even when carrying debt, find things to appreciate.

- Be grateful for what the debt enabled you to obtain (education, housing, transportation).
- Appreciate your ability to make payments and reduce balances.

- Be thankful for the learning opportunities that debt management provides.
- Recognize progress in debt reduction, however gradual.

Career and Income Gratitude

Work Appreciation

Find gratitude in your current employment situation.

- Appreciate skills you're developing or using.
- Be grateful for colleagues and professional relationships.
- Recognize the service your work provides to others.
- Appreciate the income your work generates.

Career Growth Gratitude

Approach professional development with appreciation.

- Be grateful for opportunities to learn and grow.
- Appreciate mentors and supportive colleagues.
- Recognize challenges as opportunities for development.
- Be thankful for the freedom to make career choices.

Income Gratitude

Develop an appreciation for your earning capacity.

- Be grateful for the education and experiences that enable your income.

- Appreciate the freedom that income provides.
- Recognize work as a form of contribution to others.
- Be thankful for the opportunity to earn and provide.

Overcome Gratitude Resistance

Many people resist gratitude practices because they seem inauthentic or dismissive of real problems.

Common Gratitude Objections

"Gratitude Feels Fake": When you're struggling financially, forced gratitude can feel inauthentic and dismissive of real challenges.

Response: Start with tiny, specific appreciations rather than trying to feel grateful for major areas of dissatisfaction. Appreciate small things like having clean water, a comfortable bed, or a friend's text message.

"I Don't Want to Settle for Less": Some people worry that gratitude will make them complacent and prevent them from pursuing improvements.

Response: Gratitude and ambition aren't opposites. Appreciation for what you have provides emotional stability that actually supports wise risk-taking and goal pursuit.

"Other People Have It Worse" Feels Dismissive: Using global poverty or others' problems to force gratitude can feel like dismissing your own legitimate struggles.

Response: Focus on appreciating what you do have rather than comparing your situation to others. Your problems can be real even while you simultaneously appreciate your blessings.

"Positive Thinking Doesn't Pay Bills": Practical financial stress makes gratitude seem irrelevant to actual problems.

Response: Gratitude isn't about ignoring problems—it's about maintaining emotional stability while addressing challenges. Grateful people often make better financial decisions and build stronger support networks.

Build Authentic Gratitude

Here are action steps to make gratitude real for your mindset.

Start Micro

Begin with tiny, specific appreciations.

- The taste of your morning coffee
- A comfortable temperature in your living space
- The fact that your car started this morning
- A text from someone who cares about you
- The ability to read and understand this chapter

Focus on Process

Appreciate efforts and progress rather than just outcomes.

- Be grateful for your persistence in job searching, even if you haven't found a position yet.
- Appreciate your discipline in budgeting, even if your income is still limited.
- Recognize your courage in facing financial challenges rather than avoiding them.

Appreciate Support Systems

Recognize the people and systems that contribute to your well-being.

- Infrastructure that provides electricity, water, and internet access
- People who grow, transport, and sell the food you eat.
- Teachers, ministers, mentors, and authors who have contributed to your knowledge
- Friends and family who provide emotional support

Acknowledge Growth

Appreciate your own development and learning.

- Skills you've developed over the past year
- Wisdom you've gained from challenges you've faced
- Relationships that have deepened through shared experiences
- Resilience you've built through overcoming difficulties

The Compound Interest of Gratitude

Like financial compound interest, gratitude's benefits increase exponentially over time and create positive cycles that enhance every area of life.

Personal Compound Effects

Here are more personal benefits of gratitude.

Emotional Regulation: Regular gratitude practice improves emotional stability, which enhances decision-making in all areas, including finances.

Optimism Development: Grateful people become more optimistic, which increases their willingness to take healthy risks and pursue opportunities.

Stress Reduction: Lower stress levels improve physical health, sleep quality, and mental clarity, all of which support better financial decisions.

Self-Esteem Enhancement: Gratitude builds genuine self-worth that doesn't depend on external validation or material possessions.

Relational Compound Effects

Here are more relationship benefits of gratitude.

Stronger Relationships: Grateful people attract and maintain better relationships, which provide emotional support, networking opportunities, and collaborative possibilities.

Increased Trust: Appreciation builds trust in relationships, creating opportunities for business partnerships, career referrals, and mutual support.

Generous Reputation: People known for gratitude often receive more opportunities because others enjoy working with and helping appreciative individuals.

Community Building: Grateful individuals often become catalysts for positive community development and social connection.

Financial Compound Effects

Let's outline more financial benefits of gratitude.

Better Decision-Making: Gratitude-enhanced emotional regulation leads to more thoughtful, less reactive financial choices.

Increased Opportunities: Grateful people's positive relationships and reputation often create career and business opportunities.

Reduced Impulse Spending: Appreciation for what you have reduces the compulsion to purchase items for emotional comfort.

Enhanced Creativity: Gratitude's positive emotional effects boost creativity, which can lead to innovative income generation or cost-saving ideas.

Improved Risk Assessment: Grateful people's optimism and emotional stability help them take calculated risks that can lead to financial growth.

Create Your Personal Gratitude Revolution

Developing a gratitude practice that transforms your financial life requires intentional, consistent effort tailored to your personality and circumstances.

Design Your Practice

Here are action steps to make it work for you.

Morning Gratitude Routine

- Choose a consistent time for daily gratitude practice.
- Select three to five specific items to appreciate each morning.
- Include financial blessings, however small.
- Connect gratitude to your values and goals.
- Keep a written record for reference during difficult times.

Weekly Financial Gratitude

- Review your spending with appreciation rather than judgment.
- Acknowledge progress toward financial goals.
- Appreciate people who support your financial well-being.
- Recognize opportunities available to you.
- Celebrate financial learning and growth.

Monthly Gratitude Assessment

- Evaluate how gratitude practice is affecting your financial decisions.
- Adjust practices based on what's working and what isn't.
- Set gratitude-based intentions for the coming month.
- Share appreciation with people who have supported you.
- Plan gratitude-motivated actions or generosity.

Measure Gratitude Impact

How do you know it is working? You can actually track the following so see evidence that your work is paying off.

Financial Behavior Changes

- Reduced impulse spending
- Increased satisfaction with purchases
- Better long-term financial planning
- More generous giving
- Enhanced career networking and opportunities

Emotional Well-Being Indicators

- Decreased financial anxiety
- Improved sleep quality
- Better stress management

- Increased optimism about the future
- Enhanced relationship satisfaction

Life Satisfaction Measures

- Greater contentment with current circumstances
- Reduced comparison with others
- Increased appreciation for daily experiences
- Enhanced sense of meaning and purpose
- Improved physical health and energy

The Revolutionary Nature of Gratitude

In a culture that profits from your dissatisfaction, that constantly suggests you need more to be happy, and that encourages comparison and competition, choosing gratitude is genuinely revolutionary. It's a radical act of rebellion against systems designed to keep you anxious, wanting, and consuming.

Gratitude transforms you from a consumer driven by dissatisfaction into a creator motivated by appreciation. It shifts your identity from someone who lacks to someone who has been blessed with abundance. It changes your relationships from competitive comparison to collaborative celebration.

This revolution doesn't require dramatic lifestyle changes or significant financial resources. It requires the daily choice to notice and appreciate what you already have while working toward what you want to create. It involves celebrating progress rather than obsessing over what remains incomplete. It means finding joy in the journey rather than postponing happiness until reaching an imaginary destination.

When you consistently practice gratitude, you join a quiet revolution of people who have discovered that contentment and abundance are available right now, regardless of your bank account balance. You become someone who makes financial decisions from peace rather than panic, who builds wealth through wise stewardship rather than anxious accumulation, and who experiences genuine satisfaction that no purchase can provide.

The gratitude revolution is personal but not private—its effects ripple outward, influencing everyone around you. Your appreciation becomes contagious. Your contentment becomes attractive. And your peace becomes a gift to your community. In a world full of complaints and comparisons, your gratitude becomes a beacon of possibility that lights the way for others seeking financial peace and authentic satisfaction.

This revolution begins with the simple recognition that you already have more to be grateful for than you've been acknowledging. It continues with the daily practice of noticing and appreciating those blessings. And it culminates in a transformed relationship with money, with others, and with life itself—a relationship characterized by abundance, appreciation, and authentic joy.

The gratitude revolution is available to you today, regardless of your financial circumstances, career status, or life situation. It costs nothing but attention, requires no special qualifications, and promises returns that compound daily for the rest of your life. All it asks is that you begin to notice and appreciate the abundance that's already present in your life, waiting to be acknowledged and celebrated.

Your participation in this revolution has the power to transform not just your own financial life, but the entire culture around money, success, and satisfaction. In choosing gratitude, you choose abundance. In practicing appreciation, you discover wealth that no economic downturn can threaten, and no thief can steal. This is the gratitude revolution—and it begins with your next breath, your next thought, your next choice to notice and appreciate the gifts that surround you right now.

Conclusion Chapter Ten

Perhaps no single practice is more transformative for your money identity than developing genuine gratitude for what you already have. Gratitude isn't just a spiritual feeling or feel-good emotion—it's a powerful financial tool that can literally rewire your brain's response to money and possessions. Having a grateful mindset impacts the chemicals in your brain like dopamine, serotonin, and oxytocin—which give you a sense of peace.

Complaining, on the other hand, is a waste of time because it doesn't change anything and it won't make you feel better. It affects cortisol, a stress hormone which is linked to risk of heart disease, high cholesterol, diabetes, obesity, strokes, and a weakened immune system. It can affect how your brain works, as the negative thought patterns affect the part of your brain used for problem-solving and cognitive functions. It also has negative effects on those around you.

- *Understand the privilege you have in the world. The lifestyle most of us have in America was unimaginable during Biblical times and is considered to be extremely wealthy in most parts of the world.*
- *Don't be concerned with "first-world" problems. Did your vacation not go as well as you hoped? Did you lose power for your cell phone or TV set overnight? Was the meal you ate at a restaurant not fabulous?*
- *Be thankful in all circumstances. This does not mean be thankful for all circumstances.*

When you regularly practice gratitude, the following happens.

- You become more aware of abundance in your current situation.
- You feel less compelled to acquire more to be happy.
- You make more thoughtful spending decisions.
- You experience greater satisfaction with purchases you do make.
- You reduce the anxiety and stress that often drive poor financial choices.

Gratitude practice can be as simple as regularly listing things you're thankful for, as complex as keeping a detailed gratitude journal, or as practical as pausing before purchases to appreciate what you already have.

The key is consistency. Just as negative thought patterns about money developed over time and through repetition, positive patterns must be cultivated through regular practice.

CHAPTER 11

Your Money Story Starts Here

Understanding your money identity is the first step toward financial transformation. It's the foundation for every other financial skill you'll develop and every positive change you'll make in your relationship with money.

Your current financial situation—whether it's debt, low income, lack of savings, or financial stress—doesn't define your future possibilities. Your money identity has been shaped by your past experiences, but it can be reshaped by your future choices.

The journey toward financial health begins not with a budget or a savings plan, but with an honest examination of your beliefs, emotions, and stories about money. It begins with recognizing that your worth as a person is separate from your net worth as an account holder and that financial success is possible regardless of your current circumstances or past mistakes.

This moment of beginning, or starting again, represents an extraordinary opportunity. You have decades ahead to build wealth, develop skills, and create the financial life you want. You also have the energy, adaptability, and time to make fundamental changes in how you relate to money. Most importantly, you have the chance to establish healthy financial patterns now that will serve you for the rest of your life.

Take Inventory: Where You Stand Today

Before you can change your financial trajectory, you need honest clarity about your current situation—not just your bank account balance, but your complete financial and emotional reality.

Your Financial Starting Point

These are the steps to take.

Assets and Debts Assessment

- List all your assets: bank accounts, investments, valuable possessions.
- Document all your debts: student loans, credit cards, car payments, and personal loans.
- Calculate your net worth (assets minus debts).
- Identify your monthly income from all sources.
- Track your monthly expenses across all categories.

Financial Habits Evaluation

- How do you currently make spending decisions?
- What triggers impulse purchases or emotional spending?
- How often do you check your account balances?
- Do you have any form of budget or spending plan?
- What financial goals have you set and are you actively working toward them?

Financial Knowledge Assessment

- What do you understand about investing, compound interest, and wealth building?
- How confident do you feel making financial decisions?
- Where do you currently get financial advice or information?
- What financial skills do you want to develop?

Remember, this assessment isn't about judgment—it's about clarity. Whether you're starting with significant debt, modest savings, or somewhere in between, understanding your current reality is essential for creating a realistic path forward.

Consider AF, who avoided looking at his finances for months after graduation. When he finally assessed his situation, he discovered twenty-three thousand dollars in student loans, three thousand in credit card debt, but also two thousand in a savings account and a stable job earning forty-two thousand dollars. While the debt felt overwhelming, the assessment revealed that his situation, while challenging, was manageable with consistent effort.

Your Emotional Financial Reality

It is a little different to measure your emotional mindset than it is to determine how much money is in your bank account, but the following steps will help you in this process.

Money Emotions Inventory

- What emotions do you experience when paying bills or checking account balances?
- How does your financial situation affect your mood, sleep, or relationships?
- What financial situations create the most anxiety or stress for you?
- When do you feel most confident about your financial decisions?
- What financial achievements make you feel proud or accomplished?

Money Relationship Patterns

- How do you discuss money with friends, family, or romantic partners?
- Do you hide financial information or spending from people close to you?

- How do others' financial situations affect your feelings about your own?
- What role does money play in your relationships and social activities?

Financial Identity Exploration

- How do you define financial success for yourself?
- What financial beliefs did you inherit from your family?
- How has your relationship with money changed over time?
- What financial fears or hopes shape your decision-making?

Your Values and Financial Alignment

Here are key questions to help you evaluate if there are inconsistencies between the values and purpose you have for your life and your money identity.

Core Values Identification

- What matters most to you in life beyond money?
- How do you want to be remembered by others?
- What causes, people, or activities energize and fulfill you?
- What kind of impact do you want to make in the world?
- What brings you genuine satisfaction and joy?

Current Alignment Assessment

- Does your current spending reflect your stated values?
- Are your financial goals consistent with your life priorities?
- Do your money habits support or undermine your overall well-being?
- Where do you see the biggest gaps between your values and your financial choices?

This values assessment is crucial because sustainable financial change must align with who you truly are and what genuinely matters to you. Financial strategies that conflict with your core values will feel forced and ultimately fail.

Rewrite Your Money Story

Every person has a money story—a collection of beliefs, experiences, and expectations about money that shapes financial behavior. Your current money story was written by your family, culture, life experiences, and circumstances, but you have the power to edit or completely rewrite it.

Identify Your Current Money Story

Start where you are now. Consider what may have influenced you over your life.

Family Money Messages

- What did your parents or guardians teach you about money, either directly or through their behavior?

- How did your family discuss money, finances, and economic circumstances?
- What money-related conflicts or stresses did you observe growing up?
- What financial values or fears did you absorb from your family environment?

Common family money stories include the following:

- "Money is scarce and must be carefully protected."
- "Money is the root of all evil and should be avoided."
- "Financial success requires working constantly and sacrificing everything else."
- "Other people control your financial destiny."
- "Money equals love, security, or self-worth."

Cultural and Social Influences

- What messages about money and success did you receive from your community, school, or cultural background?
- How do your peers approach money and financial decisions?
- What financial expectations does your social or professional group have?
- How do media and social media influence your financial perceptions?

Personal Experience Narratives

- What financial experiences have shaped your beliefs about money?
- What financial mistakes or successes have influenced your approach?
- How have economic conditions or life circumstances affected your financial perspective?
- What financial fears or hopes drive your decision-making?

Consider MY, whose money story was shaped by watching her parents argue constantly about finances and lose their home during the 2008 recession. Her unconscious money story became "Financial security is impossible to maintain, so why try?" This story led her to avoid financial planning and live paycheck to paycheck, perpetuating the very instability she feared.

Choose Your New Money Story

What do you want your money identity and story to be? Here are thoughts.

Identifying Limiting Beliefs

Look for money beliefs that limit your possibilities.

- "I'm not good with money."
- "Financial success is for other people, not me."
- "I'll never make enough to get ahead."

- "Money always causes problems in relationships."
- "Wealthy people are greedy or corrupt."

Creating Empowering Alternatives

Replace limiting beliefs with empowering alternatives.

- "I can learn to manage money wisely."
- "Financial success is possible for me with effort and learning."
- "I can increase my income through skill development and wise choices."
- "Money can strengthen relationships when handled wisely."
- "Wealth can be created and used for positive impact."

Writing Your New Story

Create a new money story that serves your goals and values.

- "Money is a tool that I can learn to use wisely."
- "I am capable of making financial decisions that support my well-being."
- "Financial challenges are temporary and can be overcome with persistence."
- "I can build wealth while maintaining my values and relationships."
- "My financial future is determined by my choices, not my circumstances."

Practice Your New Story

Make your new money identity stick—for lasting change.

Daily Story Reinforcement

- Begin each day by affirming your new money story.
- Make financial decisions based on your new beliefs rather than old fears.
- Challenge old thought patterns when they arise.
- Seek evidence that supports your new story.
- Celebrate progress that confirms your new identity.

Story Integration

- Align your financial goals with your new money story.
- Choose financial education and advice that supports your empowering beliefs.
- Surround yourself with people who reinforce positive financial possibilities.
- Take actions that demonstrate your commitment to your new story.
- Be patient as your new story gradually becomes your lived reality.

Set Your Financial Foundation

With clarity about your current situation and a new empowering money story, you can begin building the practical foundation for financial transformation.

Have an Emergency Fund as a Security Base

It is OK to Start Small: Begin building an emergency fund even if you can only save twenty-five dollars per month. The goal is to have at least five hundred to a thousand dollars, but it isn't entirely about the amount—it's establishing the habit and creating initial security.

Emergency Fund Benefits

- Reduces financial anxiety by providing a safety net
- Prevents debt accumulation when unexpected expenses arise
- Creates confidence to make career moves or take healthy risks
- Provides peace of mind that supports better decision-making
- Establishes saving habits that can be applied to other goals

Building Strategies

- Automate small amounts into a separate savings account.
- Save tax refunds, bonuses, or unexpected income.
- Redirect one small expense (like daily coffee) to emergency savings.
- Gradually increase contributions as your income grows.
- Celebrate milestones like reaching five hundred dollars, a thousand dollars, or one month of expenses.

Debt Management as Freedom Foundation

As I have written before, debt is regret. Debt controls you. Financial freedom comes from not being controlled by debt.

Debt Assessment and Strategy

- List all debts with balances, interest rates, and minimum payments.
- Choose between debt snowball (smallest balances first) or debt avalanche (highest interest first) approaches.
- Consider debt consolidation if it reduces interest rates or simplifies payments, but be careful with the practices of some debt consolidation companies.
- Avoid taking on new debt while paying off existing obligations.
- Focus on one debt at a time while making minimum payments on others.

Debt Mindset Shifts

- View debt payments as investments in your future freedom.
- Celebrate debt reduction progress rather than focusing only on remaining balances.
- Learn from past decisions without allowing guilt to prevent future progress.
- Recognize debt elimination as a skill that builds confidence for other financial challenges.

Avoiding Debt Trap Cycles

- Address the emotional or circumstantial factors that created the debt originally.
- Build emergency funds to prevent future debt accumulation.
- Develop spending awareness to avoid impulse debt decisions.
- Create support systems that help you stay accountable to debt reduction goals.

Basic Investment Understanding

Even with limited resources, understanding basic investment principles sets the foundation for long-term wealth building.

Time Advantage: Your greatest investment asset is time. Money invested in your twenties has decades to grow through compound interest.

Simple Starting Points

- Employer 401(k) matching (free money that should always be claimed)
- Low-cost index funds that provide broad market exposure
- Robo-advisors that automate investment management
- Target-date funds that automatically adjust risk over time

Investment Mindset Development

- View market fluctuations as normal rather than threatening.
- Focus on long-term growth rather than short-term performance.
- Understand that inflation erodes the purchasing power of money kept only in savings accounts.
- Recognize investing as participation in economic growth rather than gambling.

Starting Small: Begin investing even with minimal amounts. Many brokerages allow you to start with twenty-five dollars or less, and the habit is more important than the initial amount.

Faith and Financial Foundation

Your spiritual or philosophical worldview provides crucial context for financial decision-making and goal-setting.

Faith-Based Financial Principles

Scripture has a lot of wisdom on money principles.

Stewardship Identity: "It is required that those who have been given a trust must prove faithful" (1 Corinthians 4:2). View money management as stewardship of God's resources rather than ownership of your possessions.

Financial Foundations

- **Trust in God's Provision:** "God will meet all your needs according to the riches of his glory in Christ Jesus" (Philippians 4:19).
- **Wisdom in Planning:** "The plans of the diligent lead to profit, as surely as haste leads to poverty" (Proverbs 21:5).
- **Generosity as Priority:** "Each of you should give what you have decided in your heart to give, not reluctantly or under compulsion, for God loves a cheerful giver" (2 Corinthians 9:7).
- **Work as Calling:** "Whatever you do, work at it with all your heart, as working for the Lord" (Colossians 3:23).

Financial Integration

- Pray regularly about financial decisions and goals.
- Include tithing and generous giving in your financial planning.
- Seek wisdom through Scripture study and community.
- View career and money management as expressions of faith.
- Find accountability through church relationships and small groups.

Consider TD, who initially felt guilty about wanting financial success. Through studying biblical principles about stewardship and provision, he learned to view wealth building as responsible stewardship that created capacity for generous service rather than selfish accumulation.

Values-Based Financial Foundation

There are other values to consider in your money identity journey.

Personal Values Integration: Ground your financial decisions in clearly identified personal values rather than external expectations or cultural pressures.

Ethical Considerations

- Align investments with your environmental, social, and governance values.
- Consider the impact of your career and spending choices on others.
- Build wealth through methods that align with your principles.
- Use money as a tool for expressing your values and contributing to causes you care about.

Financial Philosophies

- **Humanistic Approach:** Focus on how money can support human flourishing, relationships, and personal growth.
- **Utilitarian Perspective:** Make financial decisions based on maximizing overall well-being and positive outcomes.

- **Existentialist Approach:** Create personal meaning around money that reflects your authentic choices and values.
- **Social Justice Focus:** Use financial resources and decisions to promote equity and positive social change.

Community and Support

- Find communities focused on financial education and support.
- Seek mentorship from people whose financial approach aligns with your values.
- Build accountability relationships that support your financial goals.
- Contribute to causes and communities that reflect your priorities.

Consider CG, who doesn't identify as religious but has strong environmental and social justice values. She structured her financial plan to include sustainable investing, supporting local businesses, and building wealth that allows her to contribute significantly to environmental causes.

Create Your Action Plan

Transformation requires moving from understanding to action. Your financial action plan should be specific, realistic, and aligned with your values and circumstances.

Short-Term Actions (Next Thirty Days)

You can do these starting now.

Immediate Foundation Steps

- Complete a thorough financial assessment (assets, debts, income, expenses).
- Open a separate savings account for an emergency fund if you don't have one.
- Set up automatic transfers for emergency fund contributions, even if small.
- List all debts and choose a payment strategy.
- Identify one area of spending to reduce or eliminate.

Knowledge Building

- Choose one financial book, podcast, or course to begin this month.
- Research basic investment options available to you.
- Understand any employer benefits (401k matching, health savings accounts).
- Learn about your credit score and how to improve it (pay on time, limit spending).
- Find reputable sources for ongoing financial education.

Mindset Development

- Begin a daily gratitude practice that includes financial blessings.

- Practice your new money story through affirmations or journaling.
- Identify and challenge limiting financial beliefs when they arise.
- Celebrate small financial wins and progress.
- Find an accountability partner or support system.

Medium-Term Goals (Next Three to Six Months)

You can accomplish the following in a few months.

Financial Structure Building

- Build an emergency fund of at least a thousand dollars, or one month of basic expenses.
- Make consistent progress on debt reduction according to your chosen strategy.
- Begin investing, even with small amounts, if you have employer matching or if your debt is manageable.
- Develop a realistic monthly budget or spending plan.
- Improve credit score through consistent payments and credit utilization management.

Skill Development

- Complete at least one comprehensive financial education resource.
- Develop confidence in making basic investment decisions.
- Learn to negotiate salary, bills, or major purchases.

- Build career skills that can increase your earning potential.
- Practice financial conversations with friends, family, or partners.

Values Integration

- Align spending with identified personal values.
- Begin or increase charitable giving within your means.
- Make career decisions that balance financial needs with personal fulfillment.
- Build relationships that support your financial goals and values.
- Find ways to contribute to your community that don't require significant money.

Long-Term Vision (One to Five Years)

You can make even more progress by considering the following ideas.

Wealth Building Establishment

- Build an emergency fund of three to six months of expenses.
- Eliminate high-interest debt (credit cards, personal loans).
- Establish consistent investing habits that will compound over decades.

- Increase income through skill development, career advancement, or side businesses.
- Consider major financial goals like homeownership, advanced education, or entrepreneurship.

Financial Independence Movement

- Develop multiple income streams or increase earning potential significantly.
- Build an investment portfolio that begins generating passive income.
- Create financial margin that allows for generous giving and opportunity taking.
- Establish expertise or reputation that creates career security and advancement opportunities.
- Develop financial wisdom that you can share with others.

Legacy and Impact Planning

- Use financial resources to make positive impacts in causes you care about.
- Mentor others in developing healthy financial habits and wealth building.
- Model financial wisdom and generosity for family, friends, and community.
- Create financial legacy that serves future generations.
- Integrate financial success with overall life satisfaction and meaning.

Overcome Common Starting Obstacles

Beginning financial transformation often feels overwhelming, especially when facing multiple challenges simultaneously.

"I Don't Make Enough Money."

Reality Check: Most wealth building happens through spending less rather than earning more. Small, consistent actions compound over time regardless of income level.

Starting Strategies

- Focus on percentage-based goals rather than dollar amounts.
- Automate savings so the amount feels manageable.
- Look for ways to increase income gradually while building habits.
- Celebrate progress rather than comparing to others with different circumstances.
- Remember that building financial skills now prepares you for a higher income later.

"My Debt Is Too Overwhelming."

Perspective Shift: Debt elimination is a skill that creates confidence and freedom. Many people have successfully eliminated significant debt through consistent effort.

Approaches

- Focus on one debt at a time while maintaining minimum payments on others.

- Consider debt consolidation if it reduces interest rates, but be cautious with what companies you use to help.
- Increase payments gradually rather than trying to sacrifice everything immediately.
- Find additional income sources specifically for debt reduction.
- Seek professional help if debt truly exceeds your ability to manage alone.

"I Don't Know Where to Start."

Start with a Simple Beginning: Start with one small action rather than trying to address everything simultaneously.

Recommended First Steps

- Track spending for one week without trying to change anything.
- Save one dollar per day for one month.
- Read one financial article or book chapter weekly.
- Set up automatic bill payments to avoid late fees.
- Have one honest conversation about money with a trusted friend or family member.

"I'm Too Young to Worry About This."

Time Advantage Recognition: Starting in your twenties and thirties provides decades for compound growth that can't be replicated by starting later.

Youth-Specific Benefits

- More time for investments to grow
- Greater ability to take calculated risks
- Higher likelihood of increasing income over time
- More energy for building new habits and skills
- Fewer financial obligations that limit flexibility

Your Story Begins Today

The most powerful moment in your financial journey is this one—the moment you decide that your current circumstances don't define your future possibilities, that your past mistakes don't prevent future success, and that you have the ability to create the financial life you want.

Your money story starts here, with this recognition that change is possible, growth is available, and financial wisdom can be learned. It starts with the understanding that your worth as a person is separate from your net worth as an account holder, but that building wealth wisely can provide security, opportunity, and the ability to contribute generously to others.

Whether you're starting with debt or savings, high income or entry-level wages, clear goals or complete uncertainty, the principles remain the same: honest assessment, empowering beliefs, consistent action, and patience with the process.

Today, there is a new set of financial challenges, but also unprecedented opportunities. You have access to information, tools, and possibilities that previous generations couldn't imagine. You also have time—decades ahead to build wealth, develop skills, and create impact.

The journey toward financial health isn't always easy, but it's always worthwhile. Each step you take toward financial wisdom creates more freedom, more options, and more ability to live according to your values. Every dollar you save, every debt payment you make, every investment you contribute builds a foundation for the life you want to create.

Your money story starts here, today, with your next financial decision. It continues with tomorrow's choices and next week's actions. It grows through months of consistent effort and years of compound returns. It culminates in a life where money serves your deepest values, supports your most important relationships, and creates opportunities for meaningful contribution to the world around you.

The first chapter of your new money story begins with these words: "I am capable of learning to manage money wisely. My financial future is determined by my faith and my choices, not my circumstances. I will build wealth while maintaining my values and relationships. My money story starts here, and it's going to be a good one."

Write that story with faith, intention, wisdom, and hope. Your future self—and everyone whose life you'll impact through your financial wisdom and generosity—is counting on the choices you make starting today.

Your money story starts here. And it starts now.

Conclusion Chapter Eleven

Understanding your money identity is the first step toward financial transformation. It's the foundation for every other financial skill you'll develop and every positive change you'll make in your relationship with money.

Your current financial situation—whether it's debt, low income, lack of savings, or financial stress—doesn't define your future possibilities. Your money identity has been shaped by your past experiences, but it can be reshaped by your future choices.

The journey toward financial health begins not with a budget or a savings plan, but with an honest examination of your beliefs, emotions, and stories about money. It begins with recognizing that your worth as a person is separate from your net worth as an account holder and that financial success is possible regardless of your current circumstances or past mistakes.

A BRIEF OVERVIEW OF BOOKS 2-5

Book 2: Overcome Money Obstacles

In the next book of the moneyhope.life series, we explore how to transform this understanding into practical steps for breaking free from financial bondage and building a healthy, sustainable relationship with money. This book goes deeper, includes tools to enact ideas and success stories:

- Weeding – Recognize and Remove the ideas and traps that keep us in financial bondage. These include: having more money makes you happy, you deserve the lifestyle you want, your work determines your worth, wealth equals success, accumulation brings peace of mind, you can't afford to be generous, credit is normal and necessary, everyone else has it figured out, money doesn't matter for relationships and financial planning is for older people.
- Seeding – Replace what doesn't work for new growth and develop financial self-awareness, have lasting

gratification, redefine wealth and success, practice contentment, build financial discipline, create new financial habits, deal with setbacks, freedom through service, keep it real with action steps along with the generosity paradox.

- Feeding – Realize new better fruits. Readers see realistic, relatable, relevant, "Your Name Here" success stories. They will be inspired by a variety of stories about overcoming circumstances – where each person replaced financial burden with peace of mind.

Book 3: Money Lies – And What to Do About Them

This book goes further. The most practical in the series, it has dozens of tools and step-by-step strategies. There are dozens of success stories – to bring readers hope.

- It starts with a reality check for what is happening to us right now, where people actually stand and where to go from here.
- The middle-class lifestyle ideal creates financial anxiety. The book covers generational, historical, political, structural and technological issues that hinder the vast majority of us.
- I disclose how entire business industries work against us – so readers are informed and prepared to protect themselves. This will help them counteract anxiety and shame so they can overcome consumer culture,

recognize financial misinformation and information asymmetry and work toward financial freedom.

- Knowing what money can do, and what it cannot do, is key to gaining financial literacy – so hopes and dreams are not misplaced, and opportunity is not wasted.
- Financial risk is not widely understood. Insurance and investment diversification are widely used to manage risk. This book makes them practical and achievable.
- Debt is regret. It is widely misused and the biggest financial obstacle to financial freedom that exists. I cover the power and danger of debt, hidden costs, how debt controls lives, and strategies to get out of debt. It clarifies what types of limited debt may be advisable as opposed to the types that cause profound problems – good debt vs. bad debt.
- What everyone should know about money is provided so readers can integrate wisdom with actions. It describes how to create your financial plan, common money challenges and mistakes, smart goals, decision making at various life stages and building resilience.
- There is a full chapter about financial emergencies – for both preparing, as well as the decision process for dealing with, an emergency circumstance in the most practical way.

Book 4: Money on Purpose

Achieving success on our own terms starts with having a profound purpose. How we live and use money affects all areas of our lives, and is an expression of our values and the lives of those around us. This book explains how having a purpose for your life is key to having a successful life. The goal is to control your money rather than being controlled by it. This book integrates and wraps up the first 3 books and includes practical tools and success stories as well.

- Find your own "why," purposeful consumption, and generosity including what to do and what not to do and how to go from your dream to having your dream job.
- Separate, clearly marked chapters provide prayers and biblical promises and explain beliefs for interested readers.
- The first scriptural assignment given to humans was to care for creation. The Ten Commandments were boiled down to loving God and loving your neighbor as yourself (our highest purpose).
- One chapter in this book is "Gods' Report Card," about how we are actually doing compared with these two purposes. Hint – not very well.

Book 5: Money Personality Relationships

Money is the reason that most marriages fail. This book is about understanding your own money personality as well as those of your spouses or partners. It describes different money personality archetypes to help people understand themselves and others who they are in relationships with. It goes further to enable people with different personalities to thrive together. I include different scenarios so people can see themselves and their relationships, in the process of improvement. The goal is to enhance both relationships and financial decisions.

BUT FIRST

Take a moment to reflect on your own money identity, acknowledge that you've already taken the most important step: you've decided to begin. What stories have you been telling yourself? What emotions drive your financial decisions? What sources have you been using to define your worth and identity?

The answers to these questions aren't meant to bring shame or judgment, but awareness and hope. Because once you understand how your money identity was formed, you can begin the process of intentionally reshaping it to serve your true well-being and deepest values.

The key is consistency. Just as negative thought patterns about money developed over time and through repetition, positive patterns must be cultivated through regular practice.

ACKNOWLEDGEMENTS

I thank God for everything. I thank my children, Amanda and Robert, as well as Tyler, for your love and inspiration. I appreciate my family, especially my sister Laura; many great friends, neighbors, colleagues; the Coachella Valley based Ophelia mentoring program including the high school girls, mentors and leadership; and my pastor. I thank you all for patiently taking time to really understand and support what I was trying to do with this project. During the process of writing this book series, your prayers, support and assistance have been profoundly helpful. The books would not exist without them.

www.ingramcontent.com/pod-product-compliance
Lightning Source LLC
LaVergne TN
LVHW030725061126
851857LV00019B/1993